MW00439403

∞

Also By Tobaise Brookins:

The Holy Spirit

F.O.R.M. P.O.W.E.R.: Forgiveness, Obedience, & Repentance Make
Prayer Overflow with Enhanced Results

The Garden Experience

Tools for Spiritual Warfare

These booklets are only available at tobaisebrookinsministries.com

OUR WARFARE

Equipping the Christian Believer for Spiritual Warfare

By

Tobaise Brookins

All Scripture quotations are taken from the King James Version of the Bible. All Hebrew and Greek notations are taken from the Strong's Exhaustive Concordance.

Our Warfare
Equipping the Christian Believer for Spiritual Warfare
Published in the United States by:
The Gates Alliance
15106 Nordhoff St. Ste 3
North Hills, CA 91343

Copyright © 2009 by Tobaise Brookins. All rights reserved Reproduction of text in whole or in part including photocopy, recording, or any information storage and retrieval system now known or to be invented, without the expressed written consent of The Gates Alliance or Tobaise Brookins except by a reviewer who wishes to quote brief passages in connection with a review written for inclusion in a magazine, newspaper, or broadcast is not permitted and is unlawful according to the 1976 United States Copyright Act.

Editorial Consultant: Bishop Ernest L. Jackson, Grace Tabernacle Community Church, San Francisco, CA.
Copy Editor: Sharon Watts, San Francisco, CA
Book Promotion & Marketing: Angela Boyce & Boyce Enterprises, Fresno, CA

Book production by: Lightning Source-an Ingram Content Company, 1246 Heil Quaker Blvd.
La Vergne, TN USA 37086

For book purchases, other resources, comments concerning the book, or speaking engagements, you may contact the author at:
tobaisebrookinsministries.com

ISBN # 978-0-578-02702-9

OUR WARFARE

Equipping the Christian Believer for
Spiritual Warfare

CONTENTS

Dedication

This book is dedicated to my loving Grandmother,

Laura Brookins.

God has used you to be the wind beneath my

wings.

FOREWORD

Christians stand front and center in the Theater of Battle where war is being waged for the soul of man. From Genesis to Revelation, the Holy Bible documents the struggle of wills—the good versus the evil; constant incursions, skirmishes, and rebellions; victories and defeats, one battle after another with short-lived peace. It will all culminate one day when God *"puts all enemies under His feet."* At that time, General Satan, his demonic cohorts and their legions, will be annihilated and cast into the Lake of Fire. This will be followed by the execution of Death and Hell, and finally the heavens and the earth will be purified from the stench of sin and evil. Until then, however, we must remember that we are at war.

Amidst all the diabolical themes in the Bible is a beautiful story about our heavenly Father who loves us so that He willingly gave His only son, Jesus Christ, to die in our stead. The great Apostle Paul puts it like this,*"God commendeth his love toward us, in that, while we were yet sinners, Christ died for us"* Romans 5:8. Satan, knowing how much God loved us, and how undeserving we were, devised a plan to take us hostage and use us as ransom in exchange for his dominance over heaven and earth. However, when Christ died for us, the Justice was paid his ransom in full by the blood of Jesus. This thwarted Satan's plan and forced him to declare war against the Church and all her members. Now every born-again believer in the Church is under attack. Once we accept Christ, we desert Satan's army and we are automatically enlisted into God's army. At stake is God's gift of eternal life—a gift worth fighting for.

Through outreach and evangelism we compel every man, woman, boy, and girl to accept Christ as Lord and Savior. During the message, we give them the *"good news"* that Jesus Christ died for their sins so that everyone that believes and accepts our message will have eternal life. Yet, we dare not broach the subject of warfare or that fact that they are enlisting in the Army of God fearing that we may lose them at the altar.

In his book, Tobaise Brookins now brings reality to the life of the Christian through a comprehensive and thorough work on spiritual warfare. He is passionate about letting every believer know that in order to *"lay hold on eternal life,"* we have to fight. You either fight or die on the battlefield. He lets us know that it is not a one-off punch here or slap in the face there, but it is a life-long battle.

All wars are fought using a strategy and Tobaise brings out the war plan God has designed for us. He conveys to the reader a battle plan for an attack as subtle as a distraction from one's prayer life to overcoming the onslaught of spiritual failure and infidelity. The theme that underpins his work is spelled out in 2 Corinthians 10:4, Ephesians 6:11, 12, and Romans 7:23, where he writes about pulling down strongholds, equipping oneself for battle, and conquering one's own personal demons—the other law in our members. He meticulously takes the reader from theory to application at the end of each chapter to make sure that what has been presented is clearly understood.

Throughout the book, he lets the reader know that one cannot be lax about their salvation. Yet, one must be constantly vigilant and on the ready—watching while praying, right hand on the Sword and left hand on the Shield—keeping our minds on Christ who equips us through His word and consoles us with His peace while we stand against the wiles of the devil.

This book cannot replace the Bible or the one-on-one conversation you will have with our Commander-in-Chief. Yet, I hope that you will be inspired, as I have, to take this book, not just a good read, but as your war manual. It has a treasure trove of spiritual information that you can use as an aid to guide you through the heat of the battle and your walk with God that will take you from earth to glory.

Bishop Ernest L. Jackson
Servant

Bishop Ernest L. Jackson is the pastor of the Grace Tabernacle Community Church in San Francisco, CA.

PREFACE

This book is long overdue. It is a labor of love and probably the most significant accomplishment of my life. There are four underlying themes that have furnished the inspiration for this book. The four themes are: Salvation is a process, supplements are not replacements, this book was an evolving work, and there is always a fight to produce. These themes underlie the inspiration of this book which makes me very confident that it will have a positive impact on you and the whole Kingdom of God.

The first underlying inspiration that prompted the writing of this book is the view that salvation is a process. I have fellowshipped with and been a part of various denominations while moving through this laboratory we call life. Yes, a laboratory, because I have found that when God wants to use you, He will first put you through some experiences and trials in life before allowing you to give truth and understanding to someone else.

Each experience and exposure to how God operates in the lives of men has provided direct data for me in my laboratory experience. God has allowed me to see the true inner workings of what it means to have a life in Him, and then freed me with the results of the experiment to give to other people. Each illumination of the word of God has brought me closer to Him and funneled me into a new experience that shows me more of who He is, which allows me to understand why He does what He does. With each experience, I move closer and closer to my ultimate salvation which is the resurrection of the body and comprehension with all saints (1 Corinthians 15, Ephesians 2). Thus, this book is an extension of the idea that God desires for His people to grow in their saved life through knowing Him. This spiritual growth starts at our entrance into the Kingdom and is cultivated and nurtured until we experience the manifestation of our complete salvation which is the rapture of the Church.

Secondly, this production of inspiration is expressed with the understanding that it is a supplement to be used in conjunction with a local church and the word of God. A valuable supplement is not a replacement of God's mandated institutes and offices. In no way should a reader think that this book by itself will be enough to move them through all of the deep dimensions of Christian life. Spiritual warfare is one aspect of a wide array of topics necessary for the child of God to master in their Christian life. This book should be used combining knowledge that comes from a Bible believing church pastor or leader, and the word of God. God has sanctioned that His word be carried by men and women who are gifted with the ability to teach the Body of Christ what His will is. Every believer should be connected with a local church. This book, television evangelism, and messages on CD or DVD should only be viewed and used as supplements that strengthen the

believer. They should not take the place of a
teacher of the word of God. No doubt, this is r
nor will it be the last book written about spiritual w...
but this may be the first and the last book that someone
reads concerning this matter. I believe that the information
contained in this book will be life changing to one, a point of
consideration for someone else, and a move to revival for
others, but it is just a part of a sea of information available to
the believer. I must also admit that a lot of restraint was used
while writing this book. I have had to use restraint because
there is some knowledge in the word of God that one must
be prepared for before gaining the wealth of power and
enlightenment contained in them. We must all crawl before
we walk, and walk before we run. This book is written with
the depth of somewhere between walking and running. Let's
just say that in this book, we will be jogging…swiftly.

The third inspiration underlying this book is that it
has evolved over time. When the Lord initially gave me the
word to produce a handbook and guide concerning effective
spiritual warfare it was called "Tools for Spiritual Warfare".
I thought that these tools were what we were supposed to
use in order to conduct spiritual warfare. I made the first
production of this concept in 1994 while studying at the
University of Washington. It was only 30 pages long. I
wrote the knowledge that God had given me in booklet
format and took it to Kinko's to self-publish. I was filled
with so much excitement. My excitement was based on my
belief that every believer needs to know the importance of
spiritual warfare and my desire to share my new found

understanding concerning the idea of children of God using "tools" to engage in war with the enemy. I passed out thousands of these small pamphlets and people were blessed. I was quite surprised by the response of people within and outside the Kingdom of God. People were encouraged and moved to become more spiritual, and take more seriously the calling that God had placed on their lives. Everywhere I preached and whenever I met with other believers, I made sure I had a few pamphlets with me.

As the years passed, the idea of "tools" began to take on another meaning. It began to settle into my spirit that one does not use tools to fight. Tools are used to make things and are products of technology used to create and progress the existence of man in a place where his necessities and amenities can be fulfilled. The *Encarta Dictionary* describes a tool as *"an object designed to do a specific kind of work such as cutting or chopping by directing manually applied force or by means of a motor"*[1]. The very definition of "tool" caused me to question the way I initially used the title: "Tools for Spiritual Warfare." After prayer, the Lord showed me that we, the children of God, are the tools used by Him to create weapons and engage in warfare. Thus, I was led to change the name of this spiritual guide to "Our Warfare", because it is designed to be somewhat of a briefing and playbook that would prepare, equip, enlighten and motivate the Christian believer to be active and effective when engaging in "Our Warfare".

---

[1] Encarta Dictionary: http://encarta.msn.com/dictionary/tool

In closing, I must admit that the illumination in this book was dispatched to me years before. God had released this body of knowledge into the spirit realm and although I received it, I didn't do anything with it. There was an internal and external fight to produce. I became stagnant and complacent, comfortable with the preaching ministry which doesn't require the same level of discipline and precision that a literary work requires. And yes, I know the Bible says, *"How then shall they call on him in whom they have not believed? And how shall they believe in him of whom they have not heard? And how shall they hear without a preacher?"* (**Romans 10:14**). Thus, my statement is not meant at all to diminish the power and relevance of preaching, but only an acknowledgement of the ease of which those of us who have been gifted to be ministry vessels in the Kingdom operate in our callings. In my humble opinion, a higher level of connection must take place between one and the revelation and truths of God in order to produce a literary work of any magnitude. And remember, the Bible also states, *"All scripture is given by inspiration of God, and is profitable for doctrine, for reproof, for correction, for instruction in righteousness"* (**2 Timothy 3:16**). Please note the emphasis on the inspiration of scripture which is the written word of God. Written information is powerful because of its ability to be reflected upon, critiqued, and meditated upon. Literature also has longevity in time that the spoken word does not enjoy.

My inability to fight through the distractions set up by the devil spun into a web of busyness that kept me from completing this work for the Kingdom much earlier. In *The War of Art*, Steven Pressfield discusses the unseen obstacles that come to all those who would attempt to be productive. In his book, he calls this unseen pressure "resistance", but we as children of God know that the accurate designation for this force is Satan. Steven Pressfield states, *"Resistance is not a peripheral opponent. Resistance arises from within. It is self-generated and self-perpetuated. Resistance is the enemy within"*[2] *pg. 8.* Completing this work for God was a monthly, weekly, and sometimes hourly battle. Reader, anytime you decide to do something for God, you will experience flesh driven and demonic resistance. I conquered this "resistance" through prayer and seeking the face of God. Finally, I was delivered into the unction necessary to complete this work. Sometimes God had to step into my life and upset my personal plans in order to get me back to doing what He wanted me to do. Therefore, this literary work is long overdue and the work of much travail, set-back, consideration, reflection, critique, and spiritual opposition.

Fighting the good fight,

Tobaise Brookins
Servant

---

[2] Pressfield, Steven. "The War of Art". Warner Books (2002). New York, NY

A TRIBUTE TO SPIRITUAL LEADERS

Apostle William T. Broadous

For being my first pastor and providing basic doctrine concerning faith, grace and servanthood. For giving an example of the power of spiritual evolution.

Bishop Roland E. Hairston

For being used to impart the truth concerning the power and person of our Lord and Savior Jesus Christ. For teaching with persuasion and providing a beginning platform for the ministry that God has given me.

Bishop Henry L. Johnson

For being my first bishop and the agent used by God to ordain me into this calling by which God so graciously has given. For being an example of integrity, spirituality, and leadership within the Body of Christ and a testimony of what a life of consecration and humility before God can bring.

Bishop Ernest L. Jackson

For embracing me as a son with open arms during life's most impactful and trying times. For being an example of endurance, excellence, and authority within the Body of Christ. For walking in integrity and preaching the unfeigned gospel with conviction and excellence.

Evangelist Louise Prince

For seeing in me the gifting that God has so graciously given. For teaching me all of the basics of evangelism, spiritual discernment, and professionalism. For being there during life's most trying times as an intercessor and channel of inspiration.

And to all of the other great leaders who have and continue to bless my life and ministry, I say, be blessed.

[15]

"For the weapons of our warfare are not carnal, but mighty through God to the pulling down of strong holds."

2 Corinthians 10:4

INTRODUCTION

This book is an expression of what I see as a continual need in the Body of Christ for Christian Education. The pool of knowledge being disseminated into the Body of Christ must be a continual process in order for the Body to be edified and equipped to harvest souls and fulfill its obligation to its Lord and Savior Jesus Christ. The wealth of information available to Christians today is quite awesome, massive, and can sometimes seem overwhelming. Yet, the available Christian resources are actually only a small fraction of the overall information available to people concerning topics that are not of God. Ungodly, demonic and humanistic materials outnumber Christian materials thousands to one, which makes this book an important asset

[17]

to the Body of Christ in our quest to live spiritual, God centered and focused lives.

Among the topics that must be covered in order to be an effective Christian, is spiritual warfare. A war is raging right now and it is imperative that every believer participate and win this war. This book is not written to be an end all of knowledge necessary to be a productive Christian. However, it is a good starting point for those who desire to be productive members in the Body of Christ and engage in spiritual warfare. It is also written to be an effective tool ministers, small groups and churches can use to further sharpen their knowledge and create powerful discussion concerning spiritual warfare. This book is a playbook.

The central theme of this book comes from a part of the powerful scripture found in **2 Corinthians 10:4** which states, ***"For the weapons of our warfare are not carnal, but mighty through God to the pulling down of strong holds."*** The Lord impressed in my spirit the power of the phrase "Our Warfare". *Our Warfare* carries us into a couple of insights from the mind of God. First, the war that is being waged is not a war of two singular enemies. This is not a fight between two men who meet in a back alley to settle a score. Satan is not God's equal. He is but a speck in the overall scheme of eternity whose only relevance is in creating an option outside of God which only magnifies the goodness, grace, and power of the only true and living God. If God wanted Satan to cease to exist, it would have been done from the beginning. Therefore, this war is a war of two kingdoms, the Kingdom of God and the kingdom of Satan. How we as children work cohesively will dictate the success we have in doing what God has called us to do. There are no lonely soldiers in God's Kingdom. We are all interconnected. There is an order and a hierarchy in place that allows God's Kingdom to always win. We are all a part of a Kingdom.

Secondly, "Our" in the key scripture does not leave anyone in the Kingdom of God out of the war. Salvation requires war. Deliverance requires war. Strengthening and victory requires war. Every spiritual gift has required war in order to be available. Our war is not a choice, it's a reality. If you don't fight, there will be a war. If you fight, there will be a war. The war is without a doubt a fact of the Christian life. The question is whether you are going to actively engage in this war or not. The war is ours. We inherited it and must fight for the duration of God's set time for us. "All hands on deck!" is the cry. Every Christian believer has been called to this war. Every denomination, ethnicity, race, and gender must be thoroughly engaged in this war. Our communities need us. Our children need us. Our nations need us. This world needs the Christian believer to engage in warfare. Our productivity in this war will be judged and the cost of not engaging in it can have devastating consequences. Therefore, we must be equipped and ready to fight the war at hand.

The key to the information in this book becoming effective in your personal life is to read it in the spirit of meditation, reflection, and interaction. The ideas in this book must have time to resonate in your spirit. Please do not read this book swiftly, but in the spirit of meditation. You may want to read one chapter at a time. You may want to read one section at a time. You may want to break the reading up into even smaller pieces. However you progress through this book, make sure you do it in the spirit of meditation. By allowing the information to have time to saturate your thoughts, you will leave this book empowered to engage in spiritual warfare. When you read a concept that captures you, consider it and pray. Allow God to have time to insulate the word within you.

Reflection is our ability to make personal connections with the text. It happens when we inject our own personal lives, experiences, and thoughts into the text. Through reflection, you will be able to analyze and synthesize this information into a meaningful experience that can be used to minister to others. This book is not written from a place of mastery and/or judgment. No one is perfect. As the author, I am not writing from a place of perfection, self-righteousness, or mastery, but a posture of humility before God, knowing that I need the words of this book as much as my fellow brother. The information in this book has had a life changing and positive impact on my life and I pray it will bless yours too. You may want to use a highlighter to note ideas in this book to reflect on. You may want to go back and re-read sections that had a strong impact within your spirit. Reflection must take place in order for the ideas in this book to become relevant, meaningful and life changing.

Finally, interact with the text. There are some issues brought to light in this book concerning the Church, leadership and the average Christian that will seem coldly harsh and sweeping at times. The voice in this book will go from being warm and inviting, to direct and reproving. At times you will feel like you are sitting on a comfortable couch in front of the fire place, listening to your loving friend share points of wisdom and knowledge with you. Other times, you will feel like you are sitting on an old cold wooden church pew, uncomfortable and challenged to reflect upon yourself and the ideas that this book confronts head on. But please understand that the information in this book is written by the inspiration of the Holy Spirit to cause us to change our focus from frivolous and wasteful spiritual living, to the importance of engaging in true spiritual warfare. The information is written with the intent to shake us up as believers. Your interaction in the content of this book will solidify you as a critical thinker concerning your religious practices and priorities as a believer. Interact by completing the activities within this book. Each chapter has activities at the end of it that are meant to create discussion, reflection and insight to the topics being presented. Discuss the information in this book with a small group or friends. By engaging in these activities, you will become more proficient in the ideas being presented and ensure yourself a life changing experience that will fortify you in spiritual warfare.

Discussions, Activities and Reflections

1. In the preface, the author describes life as a "laboratory". In what ways is life like a laboratory?

2. What lessons about war or fighting have you personally learned from life experiences?

3. How can you use your life lessons and experiences as a ministry tool to bless people?

4. Reflect on and discuss your understanding of the phrase "Our Warfare". Why is this phrase so important?

5. What are some hindrances to engaging in spiritual warfare?

Notes:

_____

_____

_____

_____

_____

_____

_____

_____

_____

"Let us make man in our image, after our likeness: and let them have dominion over the fish of the sea, and over the fowl of the air, and over the cattle, and over all the earth, and over every creeping thing that creepeth upon the earth."

Genesis 1:26

Chapter 1

EQUIPPED WITH THE HARDWARE

The raw material (hardware) necessary to be effective in spiritual warfare is already embedded in man. Believer, you are very dangerous. The hardware for power is in us all, but it takes salvation, the Holy Spirit and revelation knowledge in order for us to understand and be efficient in using the weapons we were created to make. As an ex-football player, I know how important equipment is. I can remember putting on my first football uniform. The coach gave me shoulder pads, thigh pads, knee pads and a helmet. My grandmother took me to the sporting goods store to buy cleats. No matter how fast or strong I was, I needed the equipment in order to be successful in football. The equipment protected me, but also allowed me to deliver a blow to the opponent. The equipment allowed me to play on offense and defense. Likewise, God has given mankind gifts that can only be accentuated when the equipment is used. Mankind without God will use his hardware for evil. The hardware can be devastating and destructive if used inappropriately. Yet, the hardware is taken to its full potential when it is equipped with the things of God.

One of the most powerful declarations of all scripture is found in Genesis 1:1. We read in **Genesis 1:1** the central theme of the Universe, *"In the beginning God created the heaven and the earth"*. The idea that God, all by Himself, decided to create without the coercion or persuasion of another is breathtaking. God, sitting alone, choosing to express His power and authority in such a way that eternity would be forever changed is a powerful vision to receive. Yes, the eternal, omnipotent, omniscience, self-sufficient God created. He created with the design, maturation and end product guaranteed; He being His own warranty. Our short span reality called time began with God and will end with God. In Genesis 1:1, we are not reading about the beginning of God, but rather a moment within eternity past in which God expressed a creative act. God has no beginning and has no ending. He is before the beginning, and spans into an eternity so far past our feeble understandings that to even consider it causes us to exert all of our intellectual energies; leaving us just as confused as we were when we began.

Throughout the history of mankind there have been incredible inventions and developments in technology. Egyptians built pyramids which have stood triumphant over time. Benjamin Franklin invented the bifocal, Franklin stove and the lightning rod. Benjamin Banneker invented the Farmer's Almanac and the Wright Brothers invented the first airplane. Yet with all of the inventions, discoveries and developments of man, none come close to God's pentacle creative act, "man". All of the planets and universes hang in place at the right balance and distance, with the right mix, and with just the precise ingredients to allow for life to exist on this small platform we call earth.

God created man with the ingenuity and creativity to pull out of this earth realm everything he needs in order to survive and have the standard of living of his desires. Mankind is an awesome creation. God inputs His divine programming sequence and code into man in **Genesis 1:26, 28** when He states, *"Let us make man in our image, after our likeness: and let them have dominion over the fish of the sea, and over the fowl of the air, and over the cattle, and over all the earth, and over every creeping thing that creepeth upon the earth...God said unto them, Be fruitful, and multiply, and replenish the earth and subdue it..."* This is a very powerful programming sequence. Essentially, God

[25]

established man as His agent of authority in the earth realm. God placed His pentacle creation, mankind, as authority over all His earthly creation. This explains why throughout history, man has had the ability to bring all things under his subjection. Beasts, great and small, are no match for mankind's intellect.

This has to make us feel good to know that the God of eternity decided to make us governors over all His creation in the natural realm. It must also produce a keen awareness of the responsibilities and expectations that God must have for man. Think of that Reader. The favor and trust that God has in His created man to be able to govern a huge area such as planet earth is amazing. He didn't just give man authority over the physical earth or nature, but also authority to create and govern all world systems. Mankind has been equipped with the natural hardware; waiting for God to gift him with the spiritual equipment necessary to wage war against the enemy.

Man is able to express his intelligence, creativity and dominion in the earth because of one key fact; he was made in the image of God. We note in the book of Genesis that man was created in God's image. This declaration sounds simple, but is actually a statement of conflict to the very essence of who we know God to be. Often in scripture, anthropomorphic terms *(uniquely human characteristics to non-human beings or things)* are used to describe and conceptualize the unseen eternal God. A basic study of the word of God will show us that God is an eternal, omnipresent, and omnipotent spirit that is not terrestrial in any way. Yet, man was made in His image. This means that God's creative molding was a direct reflection of how He sees Himself. The word image in Hebrew is **tsehlem** which means *resemblance, likeness, and shadowing forth*. God said that He was making man "in" His "own" image. Man then is the outline, blueprint and shadow of God's full image. Paul gleaned into this powerful revelation when he discussed the person and power of our Lord and Savior Jesus Christ stating, *"Who is the image of the invisible God, the firstborn of every creature"* (**Colossians 1:15**). Therefore, Adam is a shadow of Jesus because he was made "in" the image, but he was not the image, because Jesus "is" the image of the invisible God.

Thus, the fact that an eternal God made an image of Himself is to understand something powerful about the man He made. Man then is made with an eternal quality. This is why we read in the extension of Moses' revelation in **Genesis 2:7**, *"And the Lord God formed man of the dust of the ground, and breathed into his nostrils the breath of life; and man became a living soul."* When that which was eternal in essence (God), breathed or gave of Himself to that which was corruptible (man), it made an eternal being that has the power to govern, rule, dominate, subdue, transcend, and overcome. Yet, because man was formed with dust, he also has the ability to be corrupted, descend, fail, deceive, and live well beneath his potential.

WEAPONS OF MASS DESTRUCTION AND PRODUCTION

The idea that God wants us to be tools that make weapons of warfare is a wonderful expression of grace. Think about that. With all of our flaws and deficits, God wants to use us to make and wage war. God could just wipe Satan out with one wink of His eye, but this would open God up to accusations of being unjust and unfair. Thus, God has decided to show His power by using frail and corruptible beings to bring about eternal power and strength. We are Weapons of Mass Destruction and Production. One might say, "why not just engage in production, why destruction?" The answer is simple. Because of the constructs that Satan has set up all over this world, some things must be destroyed, before the power of God's Kingdom can become a producing force. It would be ridiculous for a construction company to start building a new housing development in between, around and on top of dilapidated homes. First the construction company must destroy the wasted homes and clear the plane before they can start building beautiful new homes.

In the years of our Lord 2001-2008, God blessed our nation with President George W. Bush who was not ashamed or afraid to call evil, EVIL. No matter what some may feel about his policies concerning healthcare, education or immigration, President Bush was a man of integrity who did not hesitate to declare who was a part of the axis of evil around the world. He also openly confessed his faith in

Christ. Being a professed Christian, it was no wonder why the mainstream media kept him under attack. I was ashamed to see even people in the Body of Christ engage in the ignorant slander of this man of faith. Although many decisions he made should have been brought under scrutiny, the level of hatred and outright disrespect for this great leader was extremely over the top which was a clear sign that Satan was mad. President George W. Bush stood boldly and declared the axis of evil which was and still is a threat to America and Christians all over the world.

During his terms, one key phrase used by his administration was "Weapons of Mass Destruction (WMD)". Weapons of mass destruction are defined as any chemical, nuclear or biological substances or weapons that can be used to destroy largely populated areas. Some would say a WMD is a weapon that can kill large numbers of humans and/or cause great damage to man-made structures (e.g. buildings), natural structures (e.g. mountains), or the biosphere in general. Troops were sent into Iraq to topple Saddam Hussein and his regime and to find weapons of mass destruction. However, the United States military was not able to find any WMD, which have caused many people to wrongly label the Iraq war a complete failure.

I too have searched for WMD and have had trouble finding any. I have traveled into many churches looking for spiritual WMD and, as the United States military, I often find none. Where are all the weapons of mass destruction in the Church? God wants to use us to destroy large bodies of demonic forces. He wants to use us to tear down demonic structures that have been in existence for far too long. He wants to use us to change whole populations from being influenced by Satan, to becoming citizens of the Kingdom of God. We need to ask the Lord to, *"teach our hands to war and our fingers to fight"* (Psalms 144:1).

Although the United States military didn't find physical weapons of mass destruction, they did help uncover some evil covert ideologies that had been brewing around the world for some time. These ideologies are actually more dangerous than the physical weapons of mass destruction because they are the root cause for the hatred found in Islamic-Fascism which breeds terrorists around the world. We too, must realize that our greatest strengths are not physical, but our beliefs that will ultimately bring down the kingdom of Satan. All the physical church buildings in the world mean nothing if they are not driven by the revelation knowledge that only God can give. With churches on every corner in some parts of our country, one would expect for our neighborhoods to be free from the violence, ignorance, abuse, and rebellion we see on a large scale. This is a sign that the church is not walking in its God given purpose. When churches don't change the communities where they are located, something is wrong.

Please note that our weapons lead to destruction and production. Anytime we destroy what should not be, we are called to replace in this world what should be. We are called to Kingdom build, just as the United States has engaged in nation building around the world to establish democracies that respect the liberties that are endowed to all human beings. After World War II, it was extremely important that the world help Japan and Germany rebuild their infrastructures, schools and economic system. Had the world left them desolate, a new Hitler would have surely risen again. Anytime there is a vacuum, the devil will seek to fill it. It is vital that the Kingdom of God be spread to and through every place in the world, both largely populated and rural. Jesus says in **Mark 16:15, "...*go into all the world and preach the gospel to every creature"*.** In other words, fill the earth with His glory. Conduct warfare that destroys when needed and produces life when needed.

The latter is a part of the significance of understanding the conquests of Joshua and the children of Israel. When God's divine and called out people finally reached the promise land, they were confused about what their quest would be. The children of Israel thought that because God promised this land to their forefather Abraham, that they would be able to just walk in and claim the land as rightfully theirs. They were sadly mistaken. By the time they entered into the Promise land, there were a lot of other nations who had taken up residence there. Jericho, Ai, Makkedah, Libnah, Lachish, Hebron and all the rest, positioned themselves to defy the sanctioned occupation of the children of Israel in the land. The children of Israel had to fight and destroy every nation that stood in their way in order to occupy the land. They were instructed by God over and over again to destroy the inhabitants and take the land.

[31]

The Lord told Joshua and the children of Israel, *"Every place that the sole of your foot shall tread upon, that have I given unto you, as I said unto Moses"* (Joshua 1:3). Note that God gave them the power to **tread**. This word tread in Hebrew is ***darak*** which means to *bend, lead, march or march forward*. Obviously, God wanted them to destroy everything in their path first, before building the kingdom that would finally come to fruition with King David, who was just a shadowing of the King of Kings who was to come much later. This treading that the Lord blessed them to be able to engage in is also seen in the words of Christ when He stated, *"Behold, I give unto you power to tread on serpents and scorpions, and over all the power of the enemy: and nothing shall by any means hurt you"* (Luke 10:19). The word **tread** used here in Greek is ***pateo*** which means to *trample* and *crush under feet*. The treading that Israel was told to do in the book of Joshua is the same treading that continues today through the Church of the Living God. We have been equipped with the ability to destroy and produce, to tear down and build up, to cut off and grow, and to establish the Kingdom of God's initiatives and power here on earth. The Kingdom is built by the King's kids, and now is the time to engage in Our Warfare.

Discussions, Reflections, Activities

1. The author makes the statement, "When churches don't change the communities where they are located, something is wrong." Discuss your thoughts about this statement. What is your church doing to make a difference in its community? What more could be done to make a difference in your community?

2. The author makes the statement, "Because of the constructs that Satan has set up all over this world, some things must be destroyed, before the power of God's Kingdom can be produced." Discuss or reflect on this statement. Then use the chart below to explore what circumstances, issues, and/or realities need to be destroyed in our lives, churches, communities and/or nation and what needs to be produced.

DESTROYED	PRODUCED

Notes:

_____
_____
_____
_____
_____
_____
_____
_____
_____
_____
_____
_____
_____
_____
_____
_____

←——————————————————————————→

"Because thou sayest, I am rich, and increased with goods, and have need of nothing; and knowest not that thou art wretched, and miserable, and poor, and blind, and naked".

Revelation 3:17

←——————————————————————————→

Chapter 2

THE CURRENT STATE OF THE KINGDOM

We are entering the last moments before the coming of our Lord and Savior Jesus Christ. The writing is on the wall, **"Mene, Mene, Tekel..."** which means *God hath numbered thy kingdom, and finished it, Thou art weighed in the balances, and art found wanting* **(Daniel 5:25).** This statement in Daniel summarizes the state of current Christendom; we are left wanting. The rapture, tribulation, Second Advent and judgment are on the way. It is time for all of us to step up to the purpose that we have been called to. We have built beautiful churches and cathedrals. We have watched the explosion of Christian television around the world. We have witnessed the exponential growth of what used to be small churches, into mega ministries, with congregations as large as twenty and thirty thousand members. Yet, with all of this apparent development, we as a body are becoming weak as it pertains to the laws and precepts of God. The result of our lack of strength in spiritual principles is seen in a variety of scandals in almost every major Christian denomination. Many political leaders who have announced their faith to the world have been prey to a wide variety of vices and behaviors not fit for the Kingdom. We are "found wanting". As we prosper naturally, we are becoming impoverished spiritually. We have learned to imitate anointing, but not walk in anointing. We have learned to mimic a powerful move of God, but never attain that power in our daily lives. We have the music, the praise leaders, the choirs, the dancers, stylish and savvy preaching, and everything else one could imagine necessary to see the power of God revealed in the midst of His people, yet, God is far from most of our services.

I have traveled the continental United States quite extensively and have witnessed the commercialization of God's anointing and word. Many church leaders have become walking infomercials, preying on the unlearned believer, the emotionally overtaken, and the simple minded. There is a lack of understanding of true ministry. Many preachers are operating in rebellion, having no sanctioning of their ministry and no authority over them. There are many who aspire for the titles of God and not the true anointing of God. Instead of waiting on God to give promotion to them, they make themselves authorities, operating in the flesh and deceiving many. In the great theological work, *Institutes of the Christian Religion*, John Calvin confronts the deficiencies within the church that are exacerbated by unsanctioned ministers who have no power to fulfill the position they have been given. Concerning the ordination practices of the Council of Chalcedon, he writes, *"But in the Council of Chalcedon it was, on the contrary, decreed that there should be no absolute ordinations, that is, ordinations without assigning to the ordained a place where they were to exercise their office...That churches may not be burdened with superfluous expense, nor idle men receive what ought to be distributed to the poor; and, secondly, That those who are ordained may consider that they are not promoted merely to an honorary office, but intrusted with a duty which they are solemnly bound to discharge"* [3]*pg. 342.* John Calvin's assessment and indictment of the church still rings true today with the lack of order and godly reasoning that defines many Christian organizations and leaders. I have listened to supposed spiritual leaders brag about their prosperity and wealth, which came from the prostituting of weak, yet sincere children of God who give faithfully, hoping that by their giving they will reach a level in God that allows them to become overcomers. Ultimately, very few of these people ever reach a level of spiritual maturity where they can move in God independently and the "Wizard of Oz" whom they called a

---

[3] Calvin, John. "Institutes of the Christian Religion"-Translated by Henry Beveridge. WM. B.Eerdmans Publishing Company (1989).Grand Rapids, MI

preacher gets to run off with the worldly esteem, social elevation, church accolade, and money.

There has also been a falsifying of God's Word and true anointing, which has led to the mimicking of power in many church conferences and meetings. People obsessed with the appearances of gifting are conducting themselves wildly and out of order in an attempt to give the appearance of a relationship with the Almighty God. False prophesies, healings, and miracles have become a staple in many large Christian meetings. If there is not a fabrication of anointing taking place, there is a lack of any anointing in other meetings. In this, we have two opposite pictures presented. First, you have a fleshly presentation of what is thought of as anointing. Secondly, you have a stale, lethargic gathering of people who claim to have the joy of the Lord but don't express any power. In both cases, there is no power.

Before His ascension, Jesus tells His disciples, *"And these signs shall follow them that believe; In my name shall they cast out devils; they shall speak with new tongues; they shall take up serpents; and if they drink any deadly thing, it shall not hurt them; they shall lay hands on the sick, and they shall recover"* (**Mark 16:17-18).** Please note that Jesus said signs "will follow them that believe". It is not God's desire that believers follow after signs, but the signs are supposed to follow believers. Yet, believers all over the world are flocking to huge meetings, hoping for a sign. Also, note that the promise given is to everyone that believes. God never intended for the believer to have to go to someone to have a demonic weight casted off of them or to learn to speak with tongues. God's power is designed for believers to be able to move in the liberty that has been purchased for them through the finished work of Christ.

Jesus has given power and authority to all believers through faith. Yet, with all of the power available, the devil has the church acting like a dog chasing his tail, going in circles and never engaging in the war that is at hand. Jesus told Peter and Andrew, *"Follow me, and I will make you fishers of men"* (**Matthew 4:19**). Jesus didn't tell them that He would fish for them. He didn't promise them a life of spiritual welfare, where they would continually have to come back to Him to get all of the basic necessities in life. Rather, He said that He would teach them, empower them, and give them the authority to be fishers themselves. The Lord promised to equip them and give them what they needed in order to be all that He foreordained them to be. The power of the Lord saying "make" must resonate strongly in our spirits, because it extends past the competence of the disciple and alters their very content. He was not saying that they would simply be good fishers because of their skill level, but rather, the content and make up of their very being would be that of a fisher. We, as a Church, have decided not to wait on the Lord's power and are therefore devising our own solutions and strategies for life's issues; suffering continual defeats. This fast-food, microwave generation is dying because our focus has shifted from true spiritual character and integrity, to one of loose and worldly pandering which is diffusing the power that should reign supreme in the Church.

This last generation Church is the same Church that the Apostle John saw in the book of Revelation. This generation is the Church of the Laodicean spoken of in **Revelation 3:14-22.** Jesus told them in verse 15, *"I know thy works, that thou art neither cold nor hot: I would thou wert cold or hot."* The church of today is neither hot nor cold. We are living in a state of compromise with the enemy. We give up our sons and daughters to drug addiction, teenage pregnancy, and disease in exchange for our form of godliness and ritzy lifestyles. This type of existence is so disgusting to God that in verse 16 He said that He would *spue* us out of His mouth. The mentality of our churches today is found in verse 17 when it says, *"Because thou sayest, I am rich, and increased with goods, and have need of nothing; and knowest not that thou art wretched, and miserable, and poor, and blind, and naked".* The rise of teachings concerning prosperity and financial wealth are wide spread. It seems like most religious leaders have been taken by the Hollywood "Lifestyles of the Rich and Famous" culture which equates success with money. Although prosperity and wealth are a part of a child of God's covenant blessings, God never desires for us to make a priority out of money or natural wealth. Money and wealth are not blessings, but the result of being blessed and obedient to Kingdom principles. Thus, to teach about money and wealth is ridiculous and out of the will of God, when holistic salvation and kingdom living is not taught as the means by which the former is manifest. Yet, ministers, "Bishops" and other spiritual leaders brag about how many members they have and fly around to conferences in private jets, signing autographs for their "fans" who buy high price Christian products that range from DVDs to attire.

To watch some of the ministers on television, you would think that the church is triumphant. Yet, many of these same preachers who house thousands of members in beautiful buildings are located in some of the most impoverished areas in the country. Their members go home to less than empowered communities; some of which don't even exist above the poverty level. But isn't it interesting that God sees us as we really are and not as we **project** we are? Jesus tells the Laodicean Church that they are *wretched, miserable, poor, blind, and naked.* Reader, I ask you, "Are you wretched, miserable, poor, blind or naked?" If you are, it is not because you don't have the power to change or effect change, and it certainly doesn't mean you are not saved. It simply means that we have allowed the devil to dupe us into putting the treasures and delicatessens of this life above the call of God. We have cleaved to the natural, rather than sought out the spiritual. Therefore, spiritual warfare is one of the topics that must be addressed in order to get the Church back in alignment with the will of God before the coming of our Lord and Savior Jesus Christ.

There are two things that must happen if the Church is to make a last stand against the wiles of the enemy. We have to build and war at the same time. We must build the Body of Christ through the glorious gospel of Jesus Christ;

calling men and women of every color, nation and creed to be saved. Then, while evangelizing the world, we must war in the spirit so that the enemy doesn't steal new babies in Christ and the Kingdom blessings freely given to all God's people. Build and war is the continuous cycle that the Church must be engaged in. What good is it to build a beautiful cathedral and the neighborhood it's in continues to be bound by spirits of violence, poverty, and lasciviousness? **Nehemiah 4:17** gives us the picture of what we have to do as believers in this last day. It says, *"They which builded on the wall, and they that bare burdens, with those that laded, everyone with one of his hands, wrought in the work, and with the other hand held a weapon."*

These mighty workers had working tools in one hand and weapons in the other hand. They were using both of their hands and all of their strength to do the will of God. They built and warred at the same time. They didn't want to build a wall, just to have the enemy come tear it down at night. That is what is happening in Christianity today. We are building in vain, because we allow the enemy to destroy everything that we have spent time, energy, spiritual and financial resources to build. I don't go to work every day just to be robbed on payday; believer neither should you. Therefore, we must make an investment in knowing who we are in God and what weapons we're created to make. God wants us to stand on our own two feet and fight the devil wherever he may try to attack. This personal commitment will become a community commitment, which in turn will become a Church wide revival that is desperately needed in this last day.

THE CURRENT PERSONAL STATE OF MANY

Another major problem among children of God is we are not heartfelt engaged in the spiritual fight that God has called us to. I heard *Bishop Henry L. Johnson* say in a sermon, *"The problem with routines is that routines can rock you to sleep. It's just like riding in the passenger seat of a car, looking out of the window. The movement of the car and scenes playing over and over often puts one to sleep."*[4] This is what has happened in the Body of Christ. We have been rocked to sleep. We have become so comfortable in the pleasure of this life that we have forgotten that there is a real fight taking place whether we decide to engage in it or not. Satan, which means *adversary*, is on his job twenty-four hours a day, seven days a week. Satan is relentless and will stop at nothing to keep men in darkness, dwarf and overthrow the plan and purpose of God for His people, and keep children of God in a defeated state. We are in a state of high alert! We are closer now than ever before to the appearing of our Lord and Savior which will ignite the rapture of His glorious Church. As we get to the end of the dispensation of grace, we must be ready and willing to step up to the challenge of spiritual warfare. The passion for the word of God is diminishing. Supplemental readings, topical CDs and DVDs have taken the place of a pure passion for reading the word of God. Some churches have bought beautiful projector

---

[4] Bishop Henry L. Johnson. "The Wait is Over". Spoken Message-paraphrased. Bishop of the 16th Episcopal District-P.A.W. Inc. (2009). Fresno, CA

screens that are an excellent multimedia resource for people, but have caused many Christians to leave their Bibles at home and sit in church with a posture of relaxation.

We hold the misconception that we decide when we go to war. My dear friend, you need to realize and internalize that the war has already begun and your enemy is serious about destroying you physically, emotionally and spiritually. Many believers walk through life continually postponing the development of their ministry. They say to themselves, "After I get back from the convention this year, I'm going to start moving in God" or, "I just need to get a few things together in my life and then I will start engaging in spiritual warfare." But the truth of the matter is, everyone is in a spiritual war whether they are cognizant of it or not. If you are a born again believer that has been sitting on the sidelines thinking that spiritual warfare is something that only high ranking ministers do, you are more than likely living in defeat. If you are a child of God who thinks that coming to church is enough to win the battle, then you are more than likely living a life beneath the covenant benefits that Christ died to provide for you. If you are a believer who has not made a commitment to Christ, you are not only in danger of being destroyed, but are hurting the Body of Christ by the absence of your gifts and talents. A lifestyle of defeat by forfeit is totally unacceptable for a child of God. God has not called us to live a life of defeat, but a life of victory in Him.

Discussions, Reflections, and Activities

1. The author gave sweeping critiques of the Body of Christ. Which statements and/or positions do you agree with? Which statements and/or positions do you disagree with? Explain.

2. What observations concerning the Body of Christ did the author miss?

3. Develop a short survey concerning the strengths and weakness of your church (minimum of 25 surveys to be conducted confidentially). Conduct the survey and document the results. Report the findings to the group and discuss the issues brought to light by the survey. If needed, put together a plan to address the areas of weakness.

Notes:

_____

_____

_____

_____

_____

_____

_____

_____

_____

_____

"But as many as received him, to them gave He power to become the sons of God, even to them that believe on his name"

John 1:12

Chapter 3

THE OVERCOMER AND THE ENEMY

In **1 John 5:4** it states, *"For whatsoever is born of God overcometh the world; and this is the victory that overcometh the world, even our faith."* The child of God should live an overcoming life. This type of overcoming is a three-fold reality that must be received by faith. First, this overcoming should permeate all areas of the child of God's life. We should live lives of overcoming in our physical, emotional, intellectual, financial, and social state, which is all a manifestation of an overcoming spiritual state. Thus, the believer should become a winner in all areas of their life and anything less than that is a compromise that is beneath the believer's privileges according to the New Covenant that our Lord and Savior Jesus Christ purchased and sealed with His own blood. All believers who are filled with the Holy Spirit have been filled with an overcoming spirit. But the object is to allow the Holy Spirit to go beyond just cleaving with our spirit, to completing the process of spiritual maturation which allows us to become pillars in the Kingdom of our God. The quickening power of the Holy Spirit, when allowed to, will download all of the mysteries of life and godliness into the spirit of the believer, so that victory becomes a daily norm and not a rarity.

Secondly, the believer should be in a constant state of overcoming. Many believers have become accustomed to a life of roller coasters, where they have victory one week, and then lose it the next. Believers all over the world have become "conference addicts", flying from one conference to the next, hoping to get their "fix". Just like a drug addict who can't go too long without getting another "hit", because their body has become dependent on the particular drugs, believers often use the church meeting in a like manner. Christians have become addicted to exaggerated assertions and emotional atmospheres that tickle the flesh but never give them the substance to affect change in their lives, ministries, communities, and nations. Christians come back from "high" services or conferences full of power and might. Then when the trials of life come, the believer once again loses the victory. We have more Christian literature available today than at any other time in the history of man. In America, an individual can literally expose themselves to 24 hour Christian programming. An individual can listen to Christian radio stations, watch Christian programming on public and cable networks, and even listen to the Word on CD. Yet, with all of this exposure to the Word of God, believers all over the world are living in defeat. Most children of God are swinging like little children on playground swings anytime the devil decides to give them a push. Believer, God expects for you and I to walk in a constant state of overcoming. In order to do this, we must be aware, tenacious, and engaged in spiritual warfare.

Thirdly, spiritual warfare allows us to overcome the world. When John says that we overcome the "world", he uses the Greek word *kosmos*, which *means the earth, the inhabitants thereof, and the world systems established against the Kingdom of God.* The world systems have been set up and established by Satan to create a demonic matrix by which humans will be inhibited from accessing the God of their salvation. This idea will be discussed further in Chapter 5, but is an important consideration in this topic. This world's system is a stratified matrix that can only be seen by a force that is able to see the whole system from outside of the system. All people in the system see the layer they exist in as a world within itself which inhibits them from seeing the larger systemic strands. For example, a drug addict is not aware of the political issues happening around the world, because their world is engulfed in the addiction they possess.   Man, outside of the salvation of God, walks through life never realizing that he and all other humans outside of the will of God are living in different arenas, levels and dimensions within a matrix that Satan has established.

Satan wants to keep the hamster, man, running on the wheel; constantly running and moving, yet never going anywhere. But God has given us the power to overcome the world. God allows the believer to see the matrix for what it is and break every system, level and dimension in Satan's kingdom. John tells us that we have overcome the world because we are born of God. Our birth in God gives us power over the world. God's children are victorious because they carry His genes. We **constantly** overcome the world which is seen in a walk of victory in all areas of the believer's life.   The word also says in **John 1:12,** *"but as many as received him, to them gave He power to become the sons of God, even to them that believe on his name:"* Note that the believer is given the power to become. The suggestion is a natural process that begins with receiving Jesus as Savior. Therefore, anyone who is born of God should live in the power of God. One cannot continually exist in defeat when they are a child of God. Victory and dominion become the common characteristics of the believer. When we receive God, power is then manifested in all aspects of our life. This should not be a reality that only takes place through a multitude of supplements such as church conventions, education and Christian media. The reality of victory is the natural flow from someone who has received God in their life. All of the matrix cords established by the enemy can be continually destroyed by the overcoming believer.

THE WHO IN YOU

What many believers never actualize is the "Who" that is inside of them. From the time you were born, the forces of this world began shaping you. Your family, culture, and society started molding you into "What" you would ultimately become. Despite the environment's pressure to shape you, God has a "Who" that He has planted inside of you. This identity was created in eternity. God says to Jeremiah, *"Before I formed thee in the belly I knew thee; and before thou camest forth out of the womb I sanctified thee, and I ordained thee a prophet unto the nations"* **(Jeremiah 1:5)**. The "Who" that God has made you is more powerful than the "What" we all feel pressured to become. In fact, God will use the natural environment in its shaping acts to give Him glory, because when God's "Who" comes out of you and takes control of the "What", it will become a testimony of how good and great our Lord and Savior Jesus Christ is. Your identity is more powerful than your calamity. This makes it all the more important for you to understand your purpose and calling. Who God made you is powerful!

The child of God should not be ignorant of what is transpiring in the spiritual realm. Child of God, you have an authentic enemy, whether you choose to acknowledge it or not, and will continually live in defeat until you confront this enemy. When you were born of the water and of the spirit you were given the ability to communicate, fight, and control happenings in the spiritual realm (*Believer, if you have not been born of the water and the spirit, it is essential that you immediately take some time to fervently pray for the new birth experience and join a Bible believing church*). Go look in the mirror. What you will see is an eagle who has probably been acting like a duck, a warrior acting like a coward, a master acting like a slave, a royal priest acting like a pagan. Look at your hands. Those hands possess the power to cast out demons, and heal all types of sicknesses and diseases. **Matthew 10:1** says, *"And when he had called unto him his twelve disciples, he gave them power against unclean spirits, to cast them out, and to heal all manner of sickness and all manner of disease."* The believer, through the authority of Christ, has power against unclean spirits and diseases. Please note that this authority was never meant to be a rarity or a unique gift, but rather the norm among believers. It should be common for us to take authority over sicknesses and devils, yet it seems that this authority is "special" in the Kingdom, for very few walk therein.

Your hands have the power to hiss the devil according to **Job 27:23** *"Men shall clap their hands at him, and shall hiss him out of his place"*. Your hands can put nations under your feet when you praise God with them. **Psalms 47:1-3 states,** *"O clap your hands, all ye people; shout unto God with the voice of triumph. For the Lord most high is terrible; he is a great King*

[51]

over all the earth. *He shall subdue the people under us, and the nations under our feet.* Our hands were made for deliverance. Our feet were made to subdue. We put fine lotion on our hands and stylish shoes on our feet, but neither our feet nor hands were made to be attractive physically or to show off the latest style. Our feet, hands, and bodies were made for dominion.

As you look in the mirror, open your mouth and examine your tongue. That tiny muscle called a tongue has the power of life and death in it. **Proverbs 18:21 states, "***Death and life are in the power of the tongue: and they that love it shall eat the fruit thereof.***"** Your tongue also holds the power through the Holy Ghost to speak mysteries. In **1 Corinthians 14:2** Paul tells the Corinthian Church, *"For he that speaketh in an unknown tongue speaketh not unto men, but unto God; for no man understandeth him; howbeit in the spirit he speaketh mysteries."* You have the power to free people who are captive and speak with the power of God; calling things that don't exist in the natural yet, out of eternity into time. Paul said, *"(As it is written, I have made thee a father of many nations,) before him whom he believed, even God, who quickeneth the dead, and calleth those things which be not as though they were"* **(Romans 4:17).** The same God that speaks into nothing and brings forth His will is the same God dwelling on the inside of you to give you the same power. However, your powers probably have not been fully utilized. A bird without wings, a tree with no leaves, and a well

[52]

without water is the spiritual state of most believers. Child of God, that is not who you were made to be, nor is it who you will become. You are loaded and dangerous! However, you are not a threat to Satan until you understand who you are and what God has ordained for you to do. You must declare yourself ready to make and use the weapons of God for *SPIRITUAL WARFARE!*

THE ENEMY

The famous book, *The Art of War* by Sun Tzu, considers the key elements of war and the most productive strategies and tactics in engaging in war. Some of the elements of war listed by Sun Tzu include how to know when an enemy is going to attack, how to position yourself before war, and how to assess the morale of your troops. One of the simplest and most profound elements of war listed is to **know your enemy.** Sun Tzu states, *"If you know the enemy and know yourself, you need not fear the result of a hundred battles. If you know yourself but not the enemy, for every victory gained you will also suffer a defeat. "If you know neither the enemy nor yourself, you will succumb in every battle"* [5]*pg. 15.* Think of his statement. You must know yourself and the enemy. If you only know yourself, you will only win half of the battles. If you don't know yourself or the enemy, you will always lose. Christians spend a lot of time in training and seminars that are geared to teach them to know who they are. I have met countless people in the Body of Christ

---

[5] Tzu, Sun. (2006). "The Art of War". Filiquarian Publishing.(2006)

who ask me questions such as, "How do I know my calling?" or "What can I do to learn more about my gifts?" Yet these questions are only one piece of the strategy in engaging in effective warfare. The other piece is to know who the enemy is, how he operates, and what strategies he has used in the past. Knowing who you are in God is powerful, but will cause you to have the same amount of victories as defeats. Thus, the object is to know yourself and your enemy.

I have noticed recently an increase in teachings in the Body that numb the believer concerning the type of enemy Satan is. These teachings that would make Satan a push-over or wimp, who is full of smoke and mirrors is very dangerous. To underestimate Satan, is similar to a man trying to cool a volcano with a common garden water hose. Knowing who Satan is and how he operates will save the believer years of frustration and move them swiftly into the abundant life that they should live. The understanding expressed by Sun Tzu is not something new. God has already declared to his people the necessity of knowing the enemy. God has admonished us that victory over the enemy first comes from knowing Him. Secondly, by knowing Him, we can then understand who we are. Thirdly, by knowing who we are, we can know who our enemy is and thereby overcome him. Knowing the enemy will keep him from having an advantage over us. Paul says, ***"Lest Satan should get an advantage of us: for we are not ignorant of his devices"*** **(2 Corinthians 2:1).**

Please understand that Satan is serious in his quest to destroy you. Therefore, you must be "strictly-business". The Body of Christ is a sleeping giant waiting to wake up and make *"the kingdoms of this world the kingdoms of our God's"* (**Revelation 11:11**). Satan absolutely abhors the very fibers of your being. He will do anything to kill, steal and destroy you. Jesus says in **John 10:10**, *"The thief cometh not, but for to steal, and to kill, and to destroy."* His sole purpose is to steal, kill and destroy. In **1 Peter 5:8** the Bible describes the devil as a roaring lion. *"Be sober, be vigilant; because your adversary the devil, as a roaring lion, walketh about seeking whom he may devour."* Note that the devil is "your adversary". No matter how you feel about him, or what deals you try to make with him, he is your adversary. Just as the United States and other nations should not negotiate with terrorist, you should not attempt to negotiate with the devil. He is dedicated to your destruction.

As stated before, the word Satan means *adversary* but that is not his name. His name is Lucifer which means *brightness; star of the morning*. He was one of God's most glorious creations until sin was found in him, according to **Ezekiel 28:11-19**. Because Lucifer aspired to exalt his throne above the stars of God and be as the Most High, he was kicked out of his position and removed from his relationship of peace with God and became a "Satan" of God and His creation **(see also Isaiah 14: 12-15)**. Jesus, God in flesh, speaks reflectively and prophetically in **Luke 10:18** when he says, *"And he*

[55]

said unto them, I saw Satan fall as lightning from heaven". Satan's fall was so dramatic that it sent the earth into a state of chaos seen in **Genesis 1:2** when Moses says, *"And the earth was without form, and void; and darkness was upon the face of the deep..."* What was once perfect in Genesis 1:1, was spun into an array of chaos that God, in His own timing, had to put back into order. The earth being without form is significant, because it expresses the fierceness of God's judgment against Satan, and the position of authority Satan had which caused such chaos. Satan's judgment becomes the template for understanding what God desires, approves of, and has a distain for.

Jeremiah also sees the fall of Satan and describes it in **Jeremiah 4:23** saying, *"I beheld the earth, and lo, it was without form, and void; and the heavens, and they had no light. I beheld the mountains, and lo, they trembled, and all the hills moved lightly."* Please note that Satan's fall was just as violent as his demeanor is toward all children of God. The war has been waging since the fall of Satan. When Satan was cast out of his position as the "Cherubim that covereth", he vowed to destroy the works of God's hand. Every being under Satan's authority suffered the same consequence of judgment. His kingdom is made up of the fallen and they all work in concert to destroy man. Satan hates everything about the believer.

The enemy's hatred of the children of God is built on two issues. One, Satan hates that man was created in the image of God, which gives man the ability to be like God. Satan wanted to be as the most high, which he was not allowed to do because God didn't make him with the ability to be or become anything outside of the position he was given. Satan's accusation against God is that God is not just and fair, because God makes all things with a specific purpose without the consent of the creation itself. You hear this argument from the lips of men and women today as they fight against the laws of God; declaring God to be inherently mean for setting things in an order without the consent of creation. Secondly, Satan hates that man has a plan of redemption, which Satan was not given. It was Satan's desire from the beginning to destroy the works of God's hand. Satan assumed that the same prescription and judgment he was given would also be given to man when he fell. But God had a different plan for man. **Romans 5:9-10** says, *"Much more then, being now justified by his blood, we shall be saved from wrath through him. For if, when we were enemies, we were reconciled to God by the death of his Son, much more, being reconciled, we shall be saved by his life."*

This plan was able to do what seemed to Satan to be impossible. It was able to declare God's absolute sovereignty and holiness, yet provide for man, who is not holy, a way to meet the standards of God's law. This plan also allowed man to keep rightful conservatorship of earth even after defaulting on the original contract. Satan was never given the power of repentance because angelic beings are made in a created state and must remain in that state for eternity.

[57]

But God has given man a plan of redemption through death and the shedding of blood, which Satan desires to make of non-effect every chance he gets. Satan is and will be our most vicious enemy until his final judgment.

Discussions, Reflections, and Activities

1. Describe the characteristics of an Overcomer.

2. The author makes the following statements, "One cannot continually exist in defeat when they are a child of God. Victory and dominion then becomes the common characteristic of the believer. When a believer receives God, power is then manifested in all aspects of their life." Reflect on these statements and express your thoughts alone, with a friend, or small group. Are these statements true? False? Explore and explain.

3. What issues or situations have kept you from experiencing the kind of overcoming discussed in this chapter?

4. This chapter talks about "The Who in You." Discuss the difference between the "What" and the "Who". Who are you?

Notes:

_____

_____

_____

_____

_____

_____

_____

_____

_____

_____

_____

_____

_____

_____

_____

_____

_____

_____

_____

_____

_____

_____

_____

"No man that warreth entangleth himself with the affairs of this life; that he may please him who hath chosen him to be a soldier."

2 Timothy 2:4

Chapter 4

COUNTING THE COST OF WAR

I have been in ministry for some time, but have not always had the same understanding of the reality of warfare as I do today. Because of misinformation given to me by various preachers, I thought that the battle was an easy one and that anyone could just pick up the battle and get the victory. I was sadly mistaken. It never dawned on me that in order to wage war with the kingdom of Satan that there would be a huge amount of risk and hurt involved. I have always been an athlete, playing football, basketball and other sports. Wanting to be a winner, I have never played a sport where I didn't exert an extensive amount of time and energy in preparing, playing and recovering. One would think that my sports background would have prepared me for the type of mentality needed in order to engage in effective warfare, but I never made the connection. Yet, after many defeats and wounds, it finally hit me: I never counted up the cost.

Dear believer, you cannot approach warfare with a desensitized perception about what is actually happening. Therefore, you must count up the cost. Jesus uses a small parable to make this point. **Luke 14: 28-30** says, *"For which of you, intending to build a tower, sitteth not down first, and counteth the cost, whether he have sufficient to finish it? Lest haply, after he hath laid the foundation, and is not able to finish it, all that behold it begin to mock him, Saying, This man began to build, and was not able to finish."* Many have been foolish enough to try to engage in warfare without first counting up the cost and devising a clear and concise strategy. This folly and ignorance has caused many to fall by the way side, being swept away by the enemy and his minions. The enemy would love for you to try to fight him without being prepared. When someone approaches the enemy undiscerning, it is a sign of ignorance or arrogance, both of which are produced by the devil himself. Note that the passage in Luke points out that success in building a tower is determined by one's ability to finish what they began. But the passage continues in **31** to say, *"Or what king, going to make war against another* *king, sitteth not down first, and consulteth whether he be able with ten thousand to meet him that cometh against him with twenty thousand?"* The king in this passage would be foolish not to have a plan to meet 20,000 men with only 10,000 men. Many children of God are trying to fight a battle that cannot be won without sufficient understanding, reinforcements, and Kingdom connections. It is essential that the believer know exactly how the enemy operates and what to bring to the battle if they expect to get the victory.

TEAM PARTNERSHIPS AND UNITY

Partnerships are extremely important in the Kingdom. Satan is given the upper hand in spiritual warfare when God's people are not unified and willing to work as partners to fulfill the common goals that God has for all His people. With so much division in the Kingdom of God, it is no wonder why the power of God is not evident in many of our churches, communities and regions. Satan's kingdom is unified and works in a cohesive manner to attain the expressed goals of Satan. God's Kingdom must work through a wide variety of social and spiritual connections in order to fulfill God's will.

Thus, when we count the cost of battle, we will most often find that we are not able to complete the battle God has called us to by ourselves. Christianity has splintered into a wide variety of denominations and beliefs that lock themselves out to one another which is exactly what Satan wants to happen. I have witnessed churches within the same denomination split to create two churches of the same denomination on the same street block. This is not of God. The strength of the Kingdom is in our ability to be unified and work as partners. Many smaller churches should pray and consider combining forces to build the Kingdom of God. There would be a combination of talents, gifts, and resources that would stand in the face of Satan's terrorist attacks on the lives of men. Satan knows what battle with him will cost and wants believers to deceive themselves into believing that the battle can be won with them alone. Believer, we must work together against the enemy. Therefore, whether Pentecostal, Apostolic, Baptist, Methodist, Full Gospel, Southern Baptist, Presbyterian, Episcopal, Catholic, Church of God, Church of Christ, Church of God in Christ, Non Denominational, Four Square, Mormon, Jehovah's Witness or any other branch that declares itself Christian, we must battle the enemy with partnerships and common initiatives that God calls us to meet. Although all Christian groups may not agree on small to large issues in doctrine or Church policy, they must find the common ground to fight the enemy on issues within their community, society and government.

When there is a need for a higher quality of education in an area, the churches in that area must band together to provide people with godly and effective services. When there are propositions on state ballots that are against the values and morals of the Kingdom of God, churches must band together to fight legislatively and spiritually against such propositions. When crime and violence plague a community, the spiritual base in that community must interconnect in order to run the devil out. Jesus addresses this issue of unity in **Luke 9: 49-50** when he says, *"And John answered and said, Master, we saw one casting out devils in thy name; and we forbad him, because he followeth not with us. And Jesus said unto him, Forbid him not:* **for he that is not against us is for us.***"* This must be the position of those in Christian leadership and the Body of Christ. We must find our commonality in order to develop strong partnerships that would become a wall against the attacks of the enemy on the lives of men and women who would come to know the Jesus as Lord.

SEVEN ENTANGLEMENTS

The Bible says in **2 Timothy 2:4**, *"No man that warreth entangleth himself with the affairs of this life; that he may please him who hath chosen him to be a soldier."* In order to be effective in spiritual warfare, you must be free of entanglements. The things that you desire to accomplish in life will only be achieved by dedication, hard work, and focus. It is easy to state that you want to achieve something. The real question becomes, are you willing to do what it takes to achieve your goal? **Proverbs 13:4 says,** *"The soul of the sluggard desireth, and hath nothing: but the soul of the diligent shall be made fat."* Many children of God simply sit around dreaming about great ministries, powerful anointing, and fulfilling their purpose, yet very few are willing to make the sacrifice necessary to make these dreams a reality. It seems that there are so many distractions presented by the devil through the world systems, human nature, and the spirit realm, that the children of God are being overwhelmed and not able to fight. We are tangled up, like a cat playing with a ball of yarn. We are tied up, like mummies prepared for death. We are unfocused, living a life of spiritual attention deficit which allows the devil to rob us, our communities and our great nation of having power with God.

In **Hebrews 12:1**, we are strongly encouraged to unwrap ourselves from sins and distractions that ultimately will stop us from running this race called Christianity. The writer says, *"let us lay aside every weight, and the sin which doth so easily beset us, and let us run with patience the race that is set before us"*. In this text, Paul points out weights and sins. A weight is not a sin, but is anything that may lead to sin, cause the believer to stumble, or drain the believer of their anointing to do the will of God. Consequently, weights can be just as deadly as sin. Weights can be carried by people for years until the death blow of sin is released which can cause death both spiritually and physically. Believers often focus on sin but not weights, or will focus on weights and not sin. We must lay aside both the sin and weights in our lives in order to be effective in the Kingdom of God. Sin creates a breach between you and God. God cannot and will not maintain a relationship with anyone or anything that is in rebellion to Him. All sin is rebellion against the laws and precepts of God and therefore puts the creation in an enemy state with the

Eternal God. This is the essence of the whole gospel message; that God has provided a way for His creation, which was in an enemy state with Him, to now attain, maintain and develop a relationship with Him.

There has been much false teaching in the Church suggesting that when one is saved, that they are free from a struggle with the flesh and sin. They continue to suggest one of two extremes. One perspective is that because we are saved by grace, there is no need for any discipline on behalf of the believer to kill the deeds of the flesh. The second is that some believe that it is possible to be perfect while in a sinful and imperfect body. Thus, they yield themselves to false pride in the self. This sets them up for failure and the faith of many is destroyed through the leaders fall. The great puritan thinker John Owen writes, *"Indwelling sin always abides while we are in this world; therefore, there is always a need for it to be mortified. Some have wrongly and foolishly believed that we are able in this life to keep the commands of God perfectly and are wholly and perfectly dead to sin...It is our duty to mortify, to be killing the sin while it is in us"* [6]*pg. 6*. This chapter will present a list of some areas in our life that can be an entanglement. These vices entangle us, which will lead to distractions that ultimately restrict us from engaging in spiritual warfare and an overcoming victory. The keynote is that weights and entanglements lead to sin. Some would

---

[6] Owen, John."The Mortification of Sin". The Banner of Truth Trust. (2004) Edinburgh, UK

debate that the entanglements below are sin, but the point the spirit is trying to express to us is that there are some things that begin in an innocent manner that can lead to bondage, strongholds, and sin that diffuse the effectiveness of the believer.

1.   Ungodly or Manipulative Relationships

Any relationships which cause individuals to be limited, restricted, or influenced against the laws, principles, or promises of God for His people are ungodly. These relationships may be with parents, children, siblings, romantic interests, spouses, co-workers, Christian peers, ministry/lay member relationships, and lay member/ministry relationships.   No matter what the relationship combination, if these relationships are founded upon ungodly premises or seeds of manipulation, an individual will never be able to engage in effective spiritual warfare. Relationships can become a focus for the children of God which will in turn cause their relationship with God to grow stagnant. Jesus said, *"No man can serve two masters: for either he will hate the one, and love the other..."* (**Matthew 6:24**). These types of relationships can be very difficult to break from because they may have generational holds on the believer which in turn will stifle a great spiritual move from taking place.   Paul says, *"Wherefore come out from among them, and be ye separate, saith the Lord, and touch not the unclean thing: and I will receive you."* (**2 Corinthians 6:17**).   In Hebrews, Paul admonishes the Hebrews to *"...lay aside every weight..."*

[67]

Therefore, the believer must unravel themselves from all ungodly or manipulative relationships so that a true and genuine relationship with God can be embraced.

2.   **Scars from Abuse that may cause Fear, Doubt, Insecurity, or Strongholds**

Often times when individuals have been abused or hurt in the past they may continue to live in an abused and withdrawn state. This abused state can inhibit them from moving into the abundant life which Christ died to provide for believers. Many people slip into depression caused by low-self-esteem or other anti-self traits. This emotional state happens most frequently with individuals who didn't receive a proper amount of validation and affirmation in younger years. Depression keeps individuals in a cycle of self degenerate emotions and ideas which restricts that person from moving forward. The believer must seek true deliverance from past abuses and traumatic experiences. The Lord will often release deliverance when the believer trusts God for deliverance and begins to move in their ministry, calling, and anointing. God wants the believer to exchange all of their "baggage" for the blessings of the Lord. *"To appoint unto them that mourn in Zion, to give unto them beauty for ashes, the oil of joy for mourning, the garment of praise for the spirit of heaviness; that they might be called trees of righteousness, the planting of the Lord, that he might be glorified"* (Isaiah 61:3).

3.   The Cares of This Life

The cares of this life are manifested in an individual engaging in excessive work which is born out of a lust and ungodly need for worldly possessions. The complexities of life often cause people to be over zealous for worldly things to meet the constant demands of our social systems. The spirit of the western world is individualistic and influences people to have an ideal of success which is against the will of God. **Mark 8:36** says, *"For what shall it profit a man, if he shall gain the whole world, and lose his own soul?"* **Matthew 6:31-33** says, *"Therefore take no thought saying, what shall we eat? Or what shall we drink? Or, Wherewithall shall we be clothed? (For after all these things do the Gentiles seek), for your heavenly Father knoweth that ye have need of all these things. But seek ye first the Kingdom of God, and his righteousness; and all these things shall be added unto you."* Note that worldly possessions are a pursuit of the Gentile (meaning heathen in this text) and that our pursuit should be for the Kingdom of God to be made manifest, which in turn, will add all of the other things to us. If you are caught in the "paper chase", you will not be able to engage in spiritual warfare.

4.   Addictions

Addictions are expressed in all types of manifestations. Many people are addicted to illegal drugs such as cocaine, crack, crystal meth, ecstasy, marijuana, and other hardcore drugs. Some people have addictions to legal drugs such as nicotine products like snuff and cigarettes, alcoholic beverages such as vodka, gin and brandy, and over the counter drugs such as pain killers, sleeping pills, and anti-depressants. Social-emotional addictions such as the need for validation, reassurance, co-dependencies, and other emotional addictions will also hinder a child of God from engaging in spiritual warfare. Virtually anything can become an addiction. The Bible encourages moderation. Yet it seems that the human spirit cannot bring itself to a moderate lifestyle without subjecting itself to a set of practices or beliefs encouraged by religions or humanist ideals.

According to a research company called Treatment 4 Addiction, "Millions of Americans succumb to the dark forces of addiction" (treatment4addiction.com). Some statistics include:

- *One out of eight Americans (27 million) is a heavy drinker or abuses illegal drugs (Source: SAMHSA)*

- *Nearly 12% of all youth consume illegal drugs by age eighteen (Source: U.S. Substance and Mental Health Services Administration)*

- *18 million Americans have an alcohol addiction problem*

- *More than 19 million individuals over the age 12 abuse illicit drugs in the U.S. (Mayo Clinic)*

- *Three percent of adults in the U.S. are classified as compulsive gamblers.*

Addictions that are less spoken about such as overeating, shopping, and laziness will also hinder the believer from moving in the power of God. Paul stated, *"And such were some of you; but ye are washed, but ye are sanctified, but ye are justified in the name of the Lord Jesus, and by the Spirit of our God. All things are lawful unto me, but all things are not expedient; all things are lawful for me,* **but I will not be brought under the power of any"** **(1 Corinthians 6:11-12).** Whether chemical, physical, or emotional, addictions are not of God and will stifle any child of God from operating in the authority rightfully theirs. Therefore, we must not allow ourselves to be brought under the power of anything outside of the Spirit of God.

5.　Unforgiveness

Unforgiveness is a very huge entanglement that if not addressed can cause the believer to live a life of unrepentence, anger, and bitterness. Unforgiveness causes individuals to be over-suspicious, pessimistic, and apprehensive in future relationships. Unforgiveness also limits an individual's relationship with God in the worst way. Jesus taught very clearly that if we do not forgive, our father in heaven will not forgive us. **Matthew 6:14-15** says, *"For if ye forgive men their trespasses, your heavenly Father will also forgive you: But if ye forgive not men their trespasses, neither will your Father forgive your* *trespasses.*" Thus, many believers are attempting to engage in ministry with unforgiven sin on their spiritual accounts. Unforgiveness of the self is also a dangerous snare. Some people are still struggling to forgive themselves for things they have done, or decisions they have made in their past that have lead to negative consequences. If we don't forgive, then we can't repent. If we can't repent, then we can never walk in the liberty wherewith God has called us. When I forgive someone, I not only loose myself up to God's forgiveness, but I also free that person from guilt. I must extend to people the graces that I have been given by God. Not only should I look to be liberated, but be a liberator. Through forgiveness, the believer can break out of the choke-hold of Satan and begin to fight with him on his own territory. If I am free, I can fight. If I am bound, I cannot fight. So the object is to be free in God, so that He can use me to engage in warfare.

6.   **A Rebellious Spirit**

This topic will be discussed in the next chapter, but I will touch upon it now. This spirit is usually the expression of selfishness, disobedience, defiance, and/or anger directed in improper manners. The seeking of attention and validation are at the root of rebellious actions. A rebellious spirit will never reach the deep things of God for it is by nature anti-God. This spirit and disposition is very dangerous because it can lead an individual to a place outside of God. Paul deals with the rebellion of previous generations and describes the process by which many fell away never to return. He states, *"And even as they did not like to retain God in their knowledge, God gave them over to a reprobate mind, to do those things which are not convenient; Being filled with all unrighteousness, fornication, wickedness, covetousness, maliciousness; full of envy, murder, debate, deceit, malignity; whisperers, Backbiters, haters of God, despiteful, proud, boasters, inventors of evil things, disobedient to parents, Without understanding, covenant breakers, without natural affection, implacable, unmerciful: Who knowing the judgment of God, that they which commit such things are worthy of death, not only do the same, but have pleasure in them that do them"* (Romans 1: 28-32).

Believers justify rebellion by claiming they have independence in God through the New Covenant. Yet, this is just a lame excuse to live in disobedience and rebellion, of which one will be held accountable for in the Judgment. Rebellion leads to disorder and exposes an individual to all the curses that exist outside of life in the Kingdom of God. When I reject God's word, I reject Him. When I reject Him, I reject life. When I reject life, I accept death. Therefore believer, explain to me how someone who is living a life leading to death, can do great exploits in God? Obviously, they can't. Therefore, rebellion must be removed from the life of the believer.

7.   **Worldliness and Excessive Participation in Social Activities. (i.e. movies, telephone talking)**

These are simple distractions that keep one from making time to communicate with God. If one is constantly on the telephone, hanging with friends, and doing social events, when do they have the time to commune with God? **Romans 13:13** says, *"Let us walk honestly, as in the day; not in rioting and drunkenness, not in chambering and wantonness, not in strife and envying."* Therefore, we should not be riotous, street wanderers, and we most definitely should not try to imitate what the world does in our lives. I've seen "Christian" shows, with people dancing around, speaking and dressing like they are on Soul Train, American Band Stand, MTV, or some Awards Show, trying to convince Christians who walk and live in the Spirit that what they are doing is the "new" thing God is doing. Believer, don't be deceived. God has not called us to be America's Next Top Model, Idol, or an MTV infomercial. We are called to be ambassadors and a chosen generation.

Even Christian activities can hinder the believer from being all they can be in God. If you are constantly at auxiliary meetings, church socials, and church outings, when will you find the time to commune with God? Constantly eating out in the name of "fellowship" can definitely become a slippery slope drawing the believer into a life of "moderate" carnality and not to a closer relationship with God. Excessive television watching can also hinder an individual from engaging in spiritual warfare. The issue

[74]

isn't so much about television as it is the gross unbalance of carnal influence over the things of God which restrict an individual's ability to engage in spiritual warfare. One must be careful how they use their eyes. **Matthew 6:23** says, *"But if thine eye be evil, thy whole body shall be full of darkness. If therefore the light that is in thee be darkness, how great is that darkness!"* Therefore, as Christians, we can have fun and enjoy life, but not at the expense of our relationship with God and our ability to be effective through Him.

These are seven examples of situations and character issues that can hinder your effectiveness in spiritual warfare. While preoccupied with these elements, you will not be focused on the battle you are engaged in. It is the trick of the enemy to get the believer to remain at a remedial place in God. Satan's tactics are three-fold. His first tactic is to keep all men and women from the knowledge of truth concerning the glorious gospel of our Lord and Savior Jesus Christ. His second tactic is to cause men and women who have accepted the call to be a disciple of our Lord and Savior Jesus Christ to fall away. And lastly, if Satan can't keep an individual from the gospel, or get them to fall away, he will try to tangle and tie-up their life with so many distractions, and bondages, that they never become an effective fisher of men or a warrior against his kingdom.

[75]

Discussions, Reflections, and Activities

1. What are the seven entanglements listed by the author?
2. Choose one of the seven entanglements and reflect on or discuss why it is so detrimental to a believer's ability to engage in spiritual warfare.
3. The Daily Schedule: Think about your average daily activities. Calculate the amount of time you spend each day praying, reading your Word, or doing spiritual activities. Reflect on your findings and consider ways to increase your participation in prayer, reading the Word, or doing spiritual things.

Notes:

_____

_____

_____

_____

_____

_____

_____

_____

_____

_____

_____

_____

_____

_____

"These six things doth the Lord hate: yea, seven are an abomination unto him: A proud look, a lying tongue, and hands that shed innocent blood, An heart that deviseth wicked imaginations, feet that be swift in running to mischief, A false witness that speaketh lies, and he that soweth discord among brethren".

Proverbs 16:16-19

Chapter 5

FIVE SATANIC FOUNDATIONAL INGREDIENTS

The foundation of Satan's kingdom is made of five ingredients; Deceit and Lies, Death by Murder, Rebellion, Fear, and Anti-God Systems. Unlike the foundations of God's Kingdom, which are fused on top of one another, Satan's foundation is mixed with the above ingredients and materials which make it difficult to know when one material begins and ends. God says, *"For precept must be upon precept, precept upon precept; line upon line, line upon line; here a little, and there a little:"* **(Isaiah 28:10)**. The Kingdom of God is organized and is the perfect expression of order. Satan's kingdom is unified, but its primary goal is to create chaos and disorder. Thus, the foundation is mixed with these five ingredients to keep one from recognizing when they are being influenced by the kingdom of Satan. There is often a lot of focus in the Kingdom of God on the legislative and moral law codes given in the dispensation of the law. Yet, the spirit behind the letter clearly shows us the motive and purpose of expressing such laws. The laws of God guard the believer from being infiltrated and destroyed by the ingredients of Satan. The Lord speaks clearly in **Proverbs 6: 16-19** stating, *"These six things doth the Lord hate: yea, seven are an abomination unto him: A proud look, a lying tongue, and hands that shed innocent blood, An heart that deviseth wicked imaginations, feet that be swift in running to mischief, A false witness that speaketh lies, and he that soweth discord among brethren"*. God hates those character flaws that are a direct expression of the enemy. The five Satanic foundational ingredients presented in this chapter encompass those characteristics that Satan's kingdom is built upon. Ultimately, all of these ingredients lead men and women to sin, which when it is done, brings forth death. Satan wants people to be separated from their creator, who is the only life source in the eternal universe.

Some men and women of God may believe that there are other characteristics that should be included in this list that the Lord has given me concerning the foundation of Satan's kingdom. In response to these discussions, I humbly submit to you that all other characteristics are the byproduct and influence of the five mentioned here. Yet, I do not want to deny anyone from exploring other characteristics and perceiving them how they may. As long as the truth of Satan is exposed and believers are able to engage in effective warfare against his kingdom, God will be glorified.

INGREDIENT ONE: DECEIT AND LIES

Deceit and lying is the most profound ingredient in the foundation because it is the essence by which we understand Satan's character, motives and actions. Jesus exposed the first and second ingredients in **John 8:44.** He states, *"Ye are of your father the devil, and the lusts of your father ye will do. He was a murderer from the beginning, and abode not in the truth, because there is no truth in him. When he speaketh a lie, he speaketh of his own: for he is a liar, and the father of it"*. This passage deals with the lying and murdering nature of Satan. He has founded his kingdom with the ingredient of deceit and lying. The ingredient of deceit and lies is the very fabric and essence of who Satan is.

From the beginning he chose not to abide in the truth. Thus, the fabric of deceit is woven so tightly in Satan's kingdom that it is literally found throughout all other characteristics. In order to wage war against Satan, you must be able to abide in the truth. Any divergence from the truth will cause you to fall into a slippery slope in which Satan will ultimately get the victory. Please note that Jesus describes Satan's lying and murdering character as being fueled by lust. Satan's fall has set the stage for bitterness and indignation to mix in a deadly potion of lust that fuels his deceitful and lusting character. He moved from believing his own lie, to becoming his own lie.

Anytime you see signs of deceit or lies in people it is always evident that Satan is roaring. Anytime people are angry, frustrated, or unresponsive to the truth, it is a sign that the enemy is working in their lives. Anytime people exaggerate and embellish facts of events, it is a sign that the enemy is working in their lives. From the earliest expressions of a lie that a baby might tell, to the more subtle lies that seemingly "good" people tell, Satan is always involved. Because God is truth, Satan desires to cause men and women to sit in a pit of deceitful lies which will keep them from being in a relationship of peace with God. Jesus points out that Satan is the father of his own lie, which means he is not influenced by any entity outside of himself when he lies and deceives. The origin of all that is untrue is Satan.

Jesus said, *"I am the way, the truth, and the life; no man cometh unto the father but by me"* **(John 4:16)**. Jesus is the truth that Satan would not abide in. The truth of Jesus' personage, identity and power is disgusting to Satan. Thus, Satan wants to imitate Christ, which is one of the milestones of any liar, imitation. Since Satan cannot be God or be in His image, he transforms himself into delusions and illusions of godliness in the sight of men. This is important to note, because many people think that they have the Holy Spirit but are really possessed and/or influenced by a demon spirit. Satan can mimic and imitate tongues and other expressions of God. Because of their past involvement with witchcraft, drugs, generational curses, and elicit behaviors, some people think that they are operating in the Spirit of God, but are being tricked by the enemy. Remember the confrontation Moses and Aaron had with the priests, sorcerers, and magicians of Pharaoh. In **Exodus 7: 10-12**, Aaron cast down his rod before Pharaoh as the Lord commanded and it turned into a serpent. This seemed to be an awesome miracle. Certainly, a rod turning into a serpent should have amazed Pharaoh, but it didn't. The priests, sorcerers, and magicians of Pharaoh threw down their rods which turned into serpents as well. Note that both the man of God and Satan's ministers had the power to change their rods into serpents. The difference was Aaron's rod swallowed the other rods. Thus, God has all power and the devil attempts to mimic that power which makes discerning the lies of Satan a full time job.

Paul grasped this revelation when dealing with the lies and deceit that many false leaders of Satan promote. Paul states, *"For such are false apostles, deceitful workers, transforming themselves into the apostles of Christ. And no marvel; for Satan himself is transformed into an angel of light. Therefore it is no great thing if his ministers also be transformed as the ministers of righteousness; whose end shall be according to their works"* (2 Corinthian 11:13-15). Note that the mimicking nature of Satan is refined and smooth, too subtle for the carnal eye to observe. But those of us who have taken up this war against Satan, must walk in discernment and expose Satan wherever his lies are promoted. This means whether his lies reside in church, organizations, people, or government, we must expose Satan's lies while abiding in the truth. It is only when he is exposed that his works can be destroyed. Without discerning Satan's lies, we will have multiple generations who exist and promote his lies. Jeremiah said, *"O LORD, my strength, and my fortress, and my refuge in the day of affliction, the Gentiles shall come unto thee from the ends of the earth, and shall say, Surely, our fathers* have inherited lies, vanity, and things wherein there is no profit. *Shall a man make gods unto himself, and they are no gods?"* (Jeremiah 16:19-20). The curse of lies and deceit that are passed from one generation to the next must be broken. It is no wonder that honesty and integrity is so difficult to find in government leaders, social workers, and spiritual leaders. Satan's lies have been passed down throughout the generations.

Satan attacked the father of faith, Abraham, with his deceit and lying motives. In **Genesis 12:10-20**, Satan wooed Abraham into convincing Sarah to lie about him being her husband. Abraham stated that Sarah should say she was his sister in order to save his life. Satan's goal was to open Sarah up to being defiled by ungodly men, thus tainting the bloodline that would ultimately lead to Christ. He wanted

God's godly seed to be mixed with the adulterous and idolatrous behaviors of the world. But God intervened and plagued the Pharaoh with great consequences which announced the danger of touching Sarah in any unclean manner. Satan also allowed for this generational curse of deceit and lying to pass through Isaac and be intensified in Abraham's grandson Jacob. Not only was this spirit on Jacob, but it was fueled by his mother Rebekah as well. Satan thought that he could subvert God's line to Christ by causing Esau's birthright and inheritance blessing to be stolen. But God used Jacob's lying spirit to put him in God's predestined will.

Satan's lies and deceit can be seen all throughout scripture and is a major ingredient of his kingdom. It is the foundation from which he conducts all of his work. This material of deceit and lying is now seen in the "Christian" world by many leaders. Never before has there been so many who speak in the name of the Lord but are secretly deceivers and children of the devil. They lie to people to gain money, wealth and fame, holding the unlearned and undiscerning bound to false promises and false doctrine. More contemporary examples are the prosperity, faith, and healing movements which have splintered, in some cases, to become cults that twist the truth of the word of God into fleshly and self-ambitious rhetoric to the gain of these fallen brothers. The lies woven into the message of many ministers are not only self-indulgent lies, but they ultimately lead to destroying the faith and souls of those who follow them.

[83]

INGREDIENT TWO: DEATH BY MURDER

The second ingredient used to promote Satan's kingdom is death by murder. Note that in the passage of **John 8:44** Jesus declares that Satan was a *"murderer from the beginning"*. There are two interesting words for "murderer" in the New Testament. The most used is a Greek word *phoneus* which means *criminal, international homicide, to slay and is connected to individual acts of murder*. It deals specifically with a general case of murder which is closely related to our contemporary understanding of murder; the unlawful killing of another. Yet the word for murderer used by Jesus is **anthropoktonos** which deals specifically with the slaying of man. This word means manslayer and is extended to encompass the murder of human beings. In **1 John 3:15**, John also uses *anthropoktonos* to stress the catastrophe of hating one's brother. John states, *"Whosoever hateth his brother is a murderer: and ye know that no murderer hath eternal life abiding in him."*

Whether someone is murdered by Satan physically, spiritually, or socially through the destruction of their reputation, murder is murder. When a homicide occurs, Satan is involved. When a little church lady slanders a person verbally around a dinner table, Satan is involved. When a new child of God is discouraged by the words or life of a more mature believer, Satan is involved. Murder is murder. This is why Jesus points out that Satan was a murderer from the beginning. Satan's deception led to the murder of the Pre-Edenic world and the Edenic world

[84]

through his own fall and by instigating the fall of Adam. Humanity was murdered by Satan; living in the natural, but not realizing they were murdered before their consciousness of death was even enlightened. It was like a murderer who puts a deadly poison in someone's drink and then walks away. When the person drinks it, they don't know that they have just taken death into their system. And although the effects of the poison may take a few minutes, an hour, or even days to take effect, the person will ultimately die, making the person who put the poison in their drink a murderer. Satan poisoned man through lust, which led to sin, causing sin to poison all humanity.

It is interesting that Jesus says the thief comes to steal, kill and destroy. The very definition of a thief is someone who steals something secretly or by open force. So why does Jesus say that this thief will go beyond stealing, into a level of killing and destroying someone? The answer to this question is very simple, but powerful as it relates to understanding the murdering nature of Satan. A thief's primary goal may be to steal, but he will ultimately kill for two reasons. The first reason a thief will kill (murder) is when what they are stealing has someone defending it. It is man's natural inclination to be dominant in the earth. It was and is Satan's desire to persuade man to consciously align with his kingdom against God. Satan's desire in the garden was to cause man to align with him, but God destroyed that plot by putting innate conflict between Satan and Man. *"And I will put <u>enmity</u> between thee and the woman, and between thy seed and her seed; it shall bruise thy head, and thou* *shalt bruise his heel"* **(Genesis 3:15).** This conflict has made it very difficult for Satan to gain humankind's deliberate allegiance. Satan knows that man has a will and would love to persuade man to willingly give up his possessions. Thus, when Satan cannot steal what he wants from man through deceit or get man to freely give it, Satan will kill to get it. This is the reason we see so many examples of good God-fearing people in politics being destroyed socially. It is not because of their behaviors, but because of their belief in God and the positions they take on various issues. Anyone who would stand against abortion, for Israel, for God's moral laws, or a wide range of other issues, will be attacked vehemently by Satan. He will use every media outlet and every imp to move against anyone who decides to stand for God and to defend the things of God.

The second reason a thief will kill (murder) is to keep the victim from ever reporting the incident. Satan then moves into a destruction mode because of all of the evidence that must be destroyed. The movement towards destruction is the natural progression in the enemy's scheme and the end result of those who follow him. He will destroy anything in his path; he has no limits or reservations concerning the destruction of anything that would keep him from his goal of blocking the plan of God. Jesus said, *"Enter ye in at the strait gate: for wide is the gate, and broad is the way that leadeth to destruction, and many there be which go in the thereat"* **(Matthew 7:13).** Murder and destruction allows for Satan to continue his arsenal of lies which work to steal from man. Once again, this reflects back to Satan's deceitful and lying character. He attempts to destroy evidence of his wickedness and then misrepresent the truth to the world, leaving humanity in darkness, confusion and away from salvation. Satan does not want anyone to ever declare him as the thief. Thus, people point the finger at each other, blame government entities and community issues without ever exposing the real entity behind all of man's negative issues; Satan.

When the enemy is confused about what God is going to do and who He is going to use, he will ultimately resort to murder. The book of Exodus records the enemy's influence on the Pharaoh to issue an executive order to kill all of the man children being born to the Hebrew women. *"And Pharaoh charged all his people, saying, every son that is born ye shall cast into the river, and every daughter ye shall save alive"* (Genesis 1:22). The enemy could tell that God's plan was in motion because of three key facts: God's people were multiplying, they were enduring and growing in spite of hardship, and they gained the favor of the Egyptian women who should have been their enemy. Child of God, when the enemy sees you multiplying, growing and receiving favor with God, he will move to destroy you and the gifting God has given you. The enemy's attempts were being thwarted which caused him to go into murder-mode, pursuing the absolute destruction of any chance for the Hebrews to have male heirs.

The enemy led Herod to issue the same type of executive ordered killing spree in Bethlehem. Satan had attacked the children of Israel for centuries, but then there was suddenly prophetic silence for over 500 years. Although battles concerning Jerusalem and surrounding areas continued to be waged, the enemy was sure that the confusion and lack of godly leadership among God's people would stunt any prophesies concerning the Christ from ever becoming a reality. But suddenly there is an announcement by Gabriel, the angel of the Lord, to a priest named Zacharias concerning the birth of a son whose name would be John, meaning Jehovah shows favor. Then there is another announcement made to a virgin girl named Mary saying, *"Hail thou that art highly favoured, the Lord is with thee: blessed art thou among women...And, behold, thou shalt conceive in thy womb, and bring forth a son, and shalt call his name Jesus"* **(Luke 1:28, 31).** The enemy saw these events rolling out and resorted to murder again by causing fear and anger to swell in the heart of Herod. *"Then Herod, when he saw that he was mocked of the wise men, was exceeding wroth, and sent forth, and slew all the children that were in Bethlehem, and in all the coasts thereof, from two years old and under, according to the time which he had diligently enquired of the wise men"* **(Matthew 2:16).** Please note the extent that Satan will go to in order to steal from man.

Currently, although silent, murders around the world have consistently increased. According to a wide variety of news and research sources, numbers as high as 6 million people are murdered each year. These numbers are modest since it is a known fact that most countries around the world don't take census data nor declare many of the genocide and ethnic cleansing on the part of various tribes and governments as murder. Also, take note of the rise in the acceptance of abortion as a justified act. Organizations such as Planned Parenthood hold intense campaigns to encourage women to choose the abortion of their heir in exchange for a perceived financial and social freedom. There is a huge push for minority and lower income women to use abortion as a birth control, which is all a part of Satan's desire to keep God's seed from entering the earth realm. The physical murders of our day are only the manifestation of the spiritual murders that are taking place on a daily basis. Remember, the enemy's ultimate goal is not to kill the physical man, but to kill the soul of man which is eternal.

INGREDIENT THREE: REBELLION

The third ingredient in the foundation of Satan's kingdom is rebellion. The spirit of rebellion is engrained in the very fiber of Satan, because it is the perspective and demeanor he holds concerning anything of God. Many Christians are deceived about their spiritual authority and power in God. They believe that spiritual gifting is the highest indicator of relationship with God. However, it is possible to have gifting and not be in an intimate relationship with God. Anyone who claims to have a relationship with God, but lives a life of rebellion, is sadly deceived and is being murdered spiritually. In *Mere Christianity*, C. S. Lewis addresses the companion of rebellion, pride, saying, *"I do not think I have ever heard anyone who was not a Christian accuse himself of this vice...The vice I am talking of is Pride or Self-Conceit; and the opposite to it, in Christian morals, is called Humility...Unchastity, anger, greed, drunkenness, and all that, are mere fleabites in comparison; it was through Pride that the devil became the devil:[7]"* pg. 103. Satan has caused many to believe that rebellion only deals with someone violating the expressed laws of God. Yet, violating an expressed law may not be rebellion, but weakness. A good definition for rebellion is *the belligerent determination one has to go against the will of God and the authorities that He has set in place.* Rebellion attempts to destroy an established authority and God hates it. **Psalms 5:10** says, **"*Destroy thou them, O God; let them fall by their own counsels; cast them out in the multitude of their transgressions; for they have rebelled against thee.*"** The individual that is in constant odds with authority has more than likely had a rebellious spirit attached to them. The individual who constantly declares their independence from the godly group or team to exercise their own will is more than likely to lunge into rebellion.

There are various words for rebellion in Hebrew, but a few help bring the detriment of this satanic ingredient to light. The first two are *pesha-to revolt,* and *pasha-to break away, quarrel, and apostatize.* Note the difference between these two words and other words such as falling, making a mistake, being weak, and disobedience through a lack of maturity. *Pesha* and *Pasha* don't suggest that the act was born

---

[7] Lewis, C.S. "The Complete C.S. Lewis Signature Classics". Harper Collins Publishers (2002) New York, NY.

out of human error or natural flaws. These words state clearly that rebellion is an act of revolt. Satan revolted against God and wanted to *break away* from his created place and position. This type of rebellion continues to be the essence that he intoxicates people all over the world with. He motivates people to want to break away from the principles and will of God. He causes them to believe the lie that they can be self-sufficient and find fulfillment without their creator. Reader, there is no fulfillment outside of God. Satan also wants the people of God to live in rebellion to spiritual authority, because he knows God absolutely despises and is disgusted with the spirit of rebellion. There is no other manifestation that is more profoundly indicative of Satan than that of rebellion.

I have witnessed extremely gifted people be totally influenced by the devil. A young man comes to mind that was and is a very gifted preacher. He is able to quote scriptures and is an unbelievable singer. Yet, every time he and I would talk, he would have something negative to say about his pastor and the decisions of other leaders in the Church. I brought to his attention his negative words and his seemingly disdain for his pastor. He looked shocked and began to try to find words to justify his rebellion. He didn't realize that God is a God of order and that He ultimately will always stand on the side of his expressed agent of authority. Watchman Nee addresses the power of authority in his powerful theological work *"Authority and Submission"*. He states, *"There are only two things that cause a Christian to lose his power. One is sin, and the other is speaking evil of those above him. The more evil speaking, the more power is lost. If a man's lack of submission is in his heart only, without corresponding utterances from his mouth, his power will not be lost as fast."* [8]

Aaron and Miriam had to learn this lesson the hard way. They allowed Satan to negatively influence them and they spoke against Moses. They thought that their rebellion against Moses was justified because of their natural relationship with Moses. But, God honors spiritual relationship to Him more than natural relationships among men. **Numbers 12:9-11** records the result of rebellion against God and His sanctioned authority. ***"And the anger of the Lord was kindled against them; and he departed. And the cloud departed from off the tabernacle; and, behold, Miriam became leprous, white as snow: and Aaron looked upon Miriam, and, behold, she was leprous. And Aaron said unto Moses, Alas, my lord, I beseech thee, lay not this sin upon us, wherein we have done foolishy, and wherein we have sinned."*** The minister with whom I spoke with didn't realize that his gifting and skill did not sanction his rebellion. The enemy was using him and was going to ultimately cause the young man to become an enemy of God.

Even infractions that seem minor are expressions of Satan's rebellion. When someone is rebellious against the policies of their employer, it is an expression of Satan. When a child is rebellious against the rules set by their parents, it is

---

[8] Nee, Watchman. "Authority and Submission. Living Stream Ministry (1988) Anaheim, CA

an expression of Satan. When someone decides to argue with established authorities such as police, teachers, and government officials, it is a direct expression of Satan's rebellious nature. Even when someone is right in an issue, the way they handle the situation will indicate whether or not they are under the influence of rebellion. The enemy always tries to get children of God to step out of their designated place of authority and operate in the spirit of rebellion. If the police officer is wrong, one should be respectful and deal with it through the channels that are in place to judge a dispute. If a teacher is wrong, a student should be respectful and go through the necessary channel to file a complaint. If a manager is not treating a child of God right, the child of God should express the love of God by enduring the hardship and being excellent in conduct and performance. Rebellion must be refrained from at all cost because it is a manifestation of demonic influence.

Another Hebrew word for rebellion is *meriy* which entails *bitterness and is a figure of rebellious.* In this definition, we see the bitterness that comes with Satan's rebellion. Because one refuses to do the will of God, they will become bitter against God. Anger, animosity and hostility are often expressed by someone who is in rebellion. This foundation in Satan's kingdom has caused a mass splitting in the Body of Christ, men and women to lose their lives, atheist to fight against any expression of Christianity, professors to openly mock Christianity, and families to break up. Satan rebelled in the beginning and continues to influence men and women to rebel against God. **1 Samuel 15:22-23** shows God's central position on this issue of rebellion. Saul was commanded to destroy all of the Amalekites and all they possessed. He decided not to kill the king and keep the possessions of the Amalekites. *"And Samuel said, Hath the Lord as great delight in burnt offerings and sacrifices, as in obeying the voice of the Lord?* Behold, to obey is better than sacrifice, *and to hearken than the fat of rams.* For rebellion is as the sin of witchcraft, and stubbornness *is as iniquity and idolatry. Because thou hast rejected the word of the Lord, he hath also rejected thee from being king."* Any child of God who does not learn that in order to have power and authority with God, that they must be able to humble themselves to obedience and flee rebellion, will constantly be defeated by Satan and live a Christian life that is unproductive. Rebellion is an expression of all that is dark and it is in this area that Satan deceives so many. He will make someone think that because they are doing something that seems good, that they are exempt from the will of God. But God honors obedience, more than any other gifts or expressions we can give him. Rebellion must be quenched in the Body of Christ if we expect to have victory against the enemy.

INGREDIENT FOUR: FEAR

The fourth ingredient in Satan's foundation is fear. Fear is toxic to the faith of the believer. Fear is the opposite of faith. The Bible uses the phrase "fear not" over a hundred and fifty times. Obviously, God had to send a word to break the bands of fear off of great leaders before they could move in Him. He tells Abraham, Hagar, Moses, Joshua, David, Solomon and countless others to fear not. Satan uses fear to hold men and women hostage to the cares of this life, the unknown, and the very God who came to save them. Through fear, Satan has caused wars to begin, nations to crumble, and people to experience all types of sicknesses. This is why the power of fear has to be destroyed through the gospel of Jesus Christ. **Hebrews 2:15** says, *"And deliver them who through fear of death were all their lifetime subject to bondage"*. This is the manifestation we see in the world today in men and women who live riotously. People who are under the spell of Satan's fear live in indecent and unbridled manners because they have no hope in a life after this life. The logic is very simple. Since there may be no tomorrow, I'll do everything I want to today. But if a man or woman is exposed to God, they will find love, which will destroy the works of fear in their life. Thus, Satan uses fear to keep people from the love of the true and living God.

John received the revelation concerning the power that fear had over people's lives. He addressed the demonic entity of fear by focusing on the love of God and how it will destroy fear. *"There is no fear in love; but perfect love casteth out fear: because fear hath torment. He that feareth is not made perfect in love"* **(1 John 4:18)**. This verse shows us that fear and love cannot be in the same place at the same time. Fear cannot remain in love. Love will always cast out fear because God's desire is for all of those who believe to be made perfect. Note that John emphasizes the inevitable connection between fear and torment. In other words, grief, anxiety, sickness, depression, and other types of physical, mental and emotional conditions are often caused by fear. Fear in relationships. Fear in money matters. Fear in career choices. Fear in future decisions. All of these expressions of fear are orchestrated and implemented by the devil himself.

Paul shows the importance of confronting and dealing with fear in many of his writings. He speaks to Timothy saying, *"God has not given us the spirit of fear; but of power, love and of a sound mind"* **(1 Timothy 1:17)**. Satan is the author of fear, not God. Even in many churches, believers are taught to live in fear. People are taught to fear the rapture, the Pastor, or a wide variety of other things. But God is not the author of fear. God is the author of liberty, because *"where the spirit of the Lord is, there is liberty"* **(2 Corinthians 3:17)**. Therefore, when you feel the winds of fear, you have to recognize that only the devil would want you to live in fear. When a person lives in fear, they become paralyzed from doing the will of God. Note that God hasn't given a spirit of fear, but of power, love and a sound mind. Power is in my spirit. Love is in my spirit and I do have a sound mind because of the spirit that is in me. Satan will do all he can to keep people in fear.

Satan uses our senses and the natural realm to create fear. Because man accesses the natural realm and human experience through his senses, Satan continually tries to get man to focus on the tangible. It is elements in the natural realm that ultimately cause fear. The complexities of life and the reality of how fragile our natural existence is, creates a lack of confidence and assurance. This intense sensation of frailty causes man to go through great lengths to protect his existence, often to the detriment of his soul. God does not commune with man through the natural environment nor man's senses. God communes with man through the spirit of man and only uses natural experiences to move man to spiritual encounters.

Take note of Paul's insight of this contrast between the body and faith. **2 Corinthians 5:6-7** says, *"Therefore we are always confident, knowing that, whilst we are at home in the body, we are absent from the Lord: (For we walk by faith, not by sight:)"*. Any presence in the body creates a natural barrier from God. This is what makes living for God while in our bodies so difficult. The body and flesh has to constantly be put under subjection in order to commune with God. Thus, Satan's kingdom exacerbates this conflict with a multitude of sensory stimuli, all designed to harden this barrier between man and God. Therefore, God bypasses this conflict and moves the believer to faith, which nullifies the spirit of fear through communion with Him. Fear is of the devil, but faith is of God.

INGREDIENT FIVE: ANTI-GOD SYSTEMS

The last material used in Satan's foundation is Anti-God systems. Anti-God systems are how the devil concretizes his character and ideals in the lives of men through the social networks man creates. A system is a set of interdependent entities working together to make a whole.

[97]

Thus, in a system, you cannot understand it by encountering one of the strands in it, but must be able to see each entity as only one piece of a larger set of connective actions. We have to see the system as a whole in order to accurately ascertain its identity, strength and influence. Because we are just individuals interacting with a wide variety of entities on a daily basis, it makes discerning an anti-God system a difficult task. The enemy then further complicates this problem of discernment by multiplying the variety and types of systems within the overall system that one has to be aware of in order to recognize his influence.

There are many different types of systems in our natural world. In Biology there is the nervous system, the digestive system, respiratory system, and circulatory system. In politics there are anarchist systems, monarchic systems, democratic systems, and theocracies to name a few. In space studies such as astronomy there are solar systems. In general sociology there are cultural systems, economic systems, educational systems, and sub-systems. All of these systems are operated by individual entities that work together. Much like these natural systems, anti-God systems have multiple entities operating in cohesion to create a whole. The only difference between natural systems and anti-God systems is that Satan is the "puppet master" pulling the strings of each layer within an anti-God system. Also note that Satan operates within all natural systems through his kingdom. Natural systems are often channels by which Satan's kingdom is expressed. Satan is involved in politics, economics, educational systems, and even the biological systems of many.

Satan first attempted to disrupt the evolution of societies in Genesis 6. As men multiplied, Satan tried to interject his seed into the physical DNA of men to create a nation of his own. The type of child that would be born from an angelic/human relationship would not be confined to all of the laws that God had set forth in his renovation of creation. God has already predestined that Jesus would be the only begotten of the father, being both God and man. Satan's desire was to create a civilization where man's ability to align with God would be compromised. Thus it reads,

> *"And it came to pass, when men began to multiply on the face of the earth, and daughters were born unto them, That the sons of God saw the daughters of men that they were fair; and they took them wives of all which they chose. And the LORD said, My spirit shall not always strive with man, for that he also is flesh: yet his days shall be an hundred and twenty years. There were giants in the earth in those days; and also after that, when the sons of God came in unto the daughters of men, and they bare children to them, the same became mighty men which were of old, men of renown. And God saw that the wickedness of man was great in the earth, and that every imagination of the thoughts of his heart was only evil continually"* **(Genesis 6:1-5).**

The multiplication of man on the face of the earth angered Satan. He is not able to duplicate himself. God made man and beast with the ability to reproduce. Satan lusted for the ability to reproduce and set up a kingdom on earth where he could exercise his authority in the earth realm the way he did during the Pre-Edenic world. The fallen angels in this passage tried to seize upon the opportunity to fulfill their lust and regain relevance in the natural realm. Before man began to organize himself in the Dispensation of Government, Satan wanted to hijack influence in the decision making process. Please note the contrast between the beginning of the passage and verse 5. Men went from multiplying, to becoming wicked. They went from being men, to being giants. The Hebrew word used for giants is *nephilim,* which means *tyrant, bully, those causing others to fall.* These fallen angels began to operate through the bodies of men in order to cause humankind to dissolve into an anti-God cesspool. It is true that man in his natural state will commit acts that are against the will of God, but the situation in this text shows how that innate weakness of man can become wickedness when the enemy is involved. Ultimately the enemy was not successful because God kept a remnant for himself in the genealogical line to Noah.

Another example of an anti-God system is Sodom and Gomorrah. The lascivious living seen in homosexuality, rape, and violent promiscuity was so heavy that God decided to destroy the whole five city system. Sodom and Gomorrah must be seen as a system. It was just two parts of a five city system. It is very significant that there were five cities in this system, because it expresses the fact that God had extended grace to them. Sodom and Gomorrah are cities representative of a social system which emphasized pleasure above productivity. It was a system of waste and violence. The homosexual acts and lascivious living of the people would never allow for them to produce children or a healthy nation. Homosexual interaction never allows for a seed to fertilize an egg. No matter where the seed is placed, there is never a designation for it to fertilize and cause reproduction. Ultimately the seed will be extracted from the body along with the rest of the waste of the body. Women who are engaged in lesbianism can only pleasure themselves, but never plant seed with each other. Thus, this system that placed sexual behavior over moral conduct and national welfare was an expression of Satan's self indulgence and careless character. It was Satan operating through man to rebel against God's commandment to be fruitful and multiply. The men of the city were ungoverned and rebellious. They were unthankful and self indulgent at the highest level. God, through Abraham, had already saved Sodom once. Years before, Abraham saved them and their goods; giving them everything that was stolen from them. Yet, their response to this act of grace by God was to allow vain and lascivious imaginations to run wild and be acted out in a manner so vile that it demanded the attention of God. The men of these cities were saved because of the righteous soul of Lot and his relationship with Abraham, yet these men constantly disrespected Lot and committed every vile deed they could.

[101]

The condition in the cities got so bad that Lot's cries reached heaven, demanding a reaction from God. **Genesis 18:20-21** records God speaking, *"And the LORD said, Because the cry of Sodom and Gomorrah is great, and because their sin is very grievous; I will go down now, and see whether they have done altogether according to the cry of it, which is come unto me; and if not, I will know"*. Although these cities were operating under an anti-God system, God still made sure that there was at least one example of righteousness in their cities, Lot. He also made sure there was an intercessor outside of the city, Abraham. Lot was God's direct response to an anti-God system and an expression of His grace. The problem with Lot was that he was not proactive in changing this anti-God system into a system that acknowledged and reverenced the true and living God. Reader, Sodom and Gomorrah could have been saved had Lot engaged in the warfare he had been called to. Contrary to popular belief, the power of God could have made Sodom into a place of peace and reverence to God. Jesus said in **Matthew 11:23** *"...for if the mighty works, which have been done in thee, had been done in Sodom, it would have remained until this day."* Lot's inability to fight in this anti-God system caused it to ultimately be destroyed. Lot became the victim, rather than the victor.

The tower of Babel was another attempt by the enemy to set up an anti-God system. This system was based on self will and man's intoxication of his own creative endowment. Nimrod and the people of this time rejected the will of God to spread all over the earth and attempted to become their own God. **Genesis 11:4** says, *"And they said, Go to, let us build us a city and a tower, whose top may reach unto heaven; and let us make us a name, lest we be scattered abroad upon the face of the whole earth"*. The people wanted to build a city in their own honor and make a tower that would memorialize them as self-sufficient and independent from the will and word of God. They also wanted to make a name for themselves. These people didn't want to scatter around the world as God had instructed humankind to do. Satan's attempt to hold dominion of earth was partly predicated on his ability to confine man both physically and in ideas. Satan wanted to establish a city similar to the one he was given authority over in the beginning before he desired to exalt his throne. Here he was again, trying to defy God. Only this time, he was doing it through the ingenuity and power of man. This is a clear example of the devil's attempt to solidify his character in a worldly system. Once again, God shut down this attempt by the devil by confusing the people's languages. It was the confusion of languages that made man scatter around the world. God wouldn't use language in this manner again until the New Testament when he used languages to unify man with His will on the day of Pentecost **(Acts 2:1-4)**. At the tower of Babel, languages scattered man. In Jerusalem, languages unified man with their God. Therefore, God destroyed these anti-God systems early in man's history, but now He requires His Kingdom to confront and defeat anti-God systems.

[103]

The Bible says, *"And be not conformed to this world: but be ye transformed by the renewing of your mind, that ye may prove what is that good, and acceptable, and perfect, will of God"* (**Romans 12:2**). The word used for conform here is **syschematizo** which means to *change one's mind or character to another's pattern.* We are admonished not to fashion ourselves after the world. The idea is to not allow oneself to be cut into a mold or pattern like the systems of this life. The transformation that must take place happens through the word of God. This transformation allows believers to prove that God's will is right. But the connection here to anti-God systems is seen in the Greek word used for "world" in this verse, *aion.* There has been much debate over this usage because it carries the meaning of *perpetual age, period of time or worlds and universe.* Some would believe that Paul's usage of *aion* here is speaking of the specific period in which the people of his day lived. Yet, there seems to be a larger framework being expressed here. These anti-God systems are all interconnected from one generation to the next. These systems are not developed for each individual generation, but they have been developed from the beginning as an expression of the enemy's character. They are strengthened by their connection to the previous generations. This is what makes anti-God systems so difficult to break and destroy. They cannot be removed by attacking the individual elements that make them or by dealing with the system that is in place for the present generation. Victory will require a high level of unified spiritual warfare that reverberates into past and future generations. The whole structure must be destroyed.

[104]

SUMMARY

These five ingredients Deceit and Lies, Death by Murder, Rebellion, Fear, and Anti-God Systems are deadly and clear signs for the believer to use when ascertaining the position and existence of the enemy. The mixing of these ingredients makes it very difficult for the natural eye to observe and analyze. It requires a high level of discernment on the part of the believer to see the progression of the enemy's kingdom in the lives of men. Inside or outside of the Church, they must be confronted and bound by the power of God. If they are allowed to fester and grow, serious individual, family, and societal consequences will continue to plague us as a believing community.

Discussions, Reflections, and Activities

1. What are the five satanic foundational ingredients?

2. What are two reasons a thief would murder someone?

3. Choose one of the ingredients in this chapter and share your thoughts.

4. What facts about these five areas did you find particularly interesting and important to understand?

Notes:

"For we wrestle not against flesh and blood, but against principalities, against powers, against the rulers of the darkness of this world, against spiritual wickedness in high places."

Ephesians 6:12

Chapter 6

SATAN AND HIS KINGDOM

Paul gives us details into the enemy's camp in **Ephesians 6:12.** The scripture reads, *"For we wrestle not against flesh and blood, but against principalities, against powers, against the rulers of the darkness of this world, against spiritual wickedness in high places."* This verse gives us a clear outline of the hierarchy of Satan's kingdom. Satan's kingdom is an organized army of all manner of spiritual wickedness whose sole responsibility is to overthrow the Kingdom of God, avert souls from being saved, and to launch continuous attacks against the Body of Christ. Satan is known by multiple names and identities. He is often called the devil (Gr. Diabolos), meaning *the slanderer* (Matt 4:1; Luke 4:2; John 8:44; Eph 6:11; Rev 12:12). Please also note that the term *devils* in the King James Version and ERV is properly written *demons*. Other titles or descriptive designations applied to Satan are "Abaddon" or "Apollyon" (Rev 9:11); "Accuser of our brothers" (12:10); "enemy," Greek *antidikos* (1 Peter 5:8); "Beelzebub" (Matt 12:24); "Belial" (2 Cor 6:15); the one who "leads the whole world astray" (Rev 12:9); "the evil one" (Matt 13:19, 38; 1 John 2:13; 5:19); "the father of lies" (John 8:44); "the god of this age" (2 Cor 4:4; "a murderer" (John 8:44); "that ancient serpent" Rev 12:9); "the prince of this world" (John 12:31; 14:30); "the ruler of the kingdom of the air" (Eph 2:2); "the tempter" (Matt 4:5; 1 Thess 3:5).[9] All of these descriptive designations give us clarity of the type of enemy Satan is.

WE WRESTLE

First, Paul describes the relationship between the believer and the kingdom of Satan. Paul says in **Ephesians 6:12**, "For we wrestle". The Greek word for "wrestle" is a compound word, **eimit-pale**. *Eimit* means *to be* or *present*, denoting the current and on-going war we are engaged in.

---

[9] Douglas, J.D., Tenney, Merrill C., "The New International Dictionary of the Bible Pictorial Edition". The Zondervan Publishing House (1987) Grand Rapids, MI

The word *pale* means *to struggle.* Thus, wrestle in this context means to *struggle, fight, to contend by grappling, hand to hand combat in the indefinite present.* This struggle is hand to hand and current. Not current one time, but indefinitely. There is no revealed time set for our war to end. Only God knows the day and hour when the rapture will take place. Believer, this battle is a struggle that must take place constantly. We must be cognizant of our war every day, hour and minute. We are contending in a war that has high rewards for the winner and much to lose for the defeated.

Another way to understand the type of warfare or wrestling that we are a part of is to think of guerilla warfare. Guerilla Warfare became highly publicized during the Vietnam War. The military strength of the United States far surpassed that of the North Vietnamese. The U.S. Air Force, Navy, and Marines could have wiped the whole region clean, but they did not want to kill civilians while attempting to kill armed enemy soldiers. This made the U.S. forces have to engage in Guerilla Warfare which evened the playing field with their much inferior enemy. The enemy was very familiar with the jungle, forest, and terrain of Vietnam which gave them a substantial advantage over the U.S. soldiers. The enemy also had a different philosophy for life and war. The enemy was not concerned about the death of women and children, and would even use women and children to lure the U.S. soldiers into traps which cost many their lives. Hand to hand combat is a long and arduous process that ultimately keeps a soldier on the edge emotionally and mentally; knowing that at any time an attack could ensue and they could be killed. Believer, we are in the same type of wrestling warfare. We must be ready at all times. We must be on the edge spiritually; ready to attack and always expecting to be attacked. We must be acutely aware of the war at hand and fight with all persistence and resolve.

When engaged in spiritual warfare, we must know what and who we are fighting against. The higher the demonic level, the higher level of power is required to affect change in that particular spiritual dimension. As we move into new levels of spiritual maturity and dimension, more strength, focus and discipline will be required. Even the disciples were shocked to find out that the authority that they were walking in was not enough to cast out the lunatic demon in **Matthew 17:14-21.** Jesus told his disciples, *"Howbeit this kind goeth not out but by prayer and fasting"*. The disciples' assumption was that their relationship with Christ was enough to give them complete authority. They were wrong. A relationship with Christ must be nurtured and developed so that one's spiritual senses are strengthened and sharpened. Therefore, we must make sure we are fully equipped spiritually in order to affect change in the spiritual realm.

FLESH AND BLOOD

Paul's phrase in **Ephesians 6:12**, "not against flesh and blood" makes us aware that the war we are fighting is not natural. There has been much literature published and many great speeches/sermons presented emphasizing this fact to believers. Yet, with all of the discussion concerning this fact, our actions as believers show that we have not truly taken to heart the reality and the power of this phrase. As a body, we continue to act through our natural strength. We brag about what "We" have done, and in a back handed kind of way say, "To God be the Glory" at the end of our rant of self promotion. Preachers brag about what they are doing to gain new members. Conferences are held concerning what any individual can do to be a great leader and build a successful ministry; all of which focus on business models that have simply been given a new Christian name to attract believers. Yet, your understanding of the uselessness of the flesh will be the deciding factor between victory and defeat. If I do it according to the flesh, I will lose. If I engage in battle according to the spirit, I will win.

Despite the negative feelings we may hold about people such as our parents, associates, school teachers or co-workers, they are not our real enemy. Our enemy is not a nation, company, or people. The reality is we are not fighting against any humans or anything natural at all. We are actually warring against the demon spirits who motivate people to create adverse situations. The biggest mistake a child of God can make is to constantly try to affect change in the natural realm by only doing natural things. Only natural actions connected to spiritual authority will affect true change. Natural actions have natural consequences, but spiritual actions can alter natural actions which lead to natural consequences. Constantly debating, arguing, and attempting to change elements of the natural realm through physical strength and violence is useless. The battle we fight is a spiritual battle and therefore must be fought in the spirit. Everything in the natural realm has a spiritual root as its foundation and must therefore be dealt with in the spirit.

Hebrews 11:3 says, *"Through faith we understand that the worlds were framed by the word of God, so that things which are seen were not made of things which do appear."* This passage allows us to understand that all things tangible and intangible were formed by that which is spirit. Thus, the eternal Spirit (God) created all things by His word, which is the expression of His creative design. We have power to change anything in the natural realm by attacking it at the root. Poverty is not just a natural reality that some people face, but a spirit. Sickness is not always just a natural reality, but is often times influenced by a spirit. Crime, rebellion, jealousy, and even addictions have spiritual foundations and must therefore be confronted in the spirit. This is also true of spiritual blessings; they must be accepted in the spirit first. Therefore, if I can war in the spirit, I can change the natural. If I can't war in the spirit, then I will be cursed to live a life waiting to respond to circumstances in the natural that I can't control.

I used to have a huge ugly tree in my front yard. In order to get rid of the tree I had two choices. One, I could cut all the branches down and the trunk of the tree until it was at ground level. This way, it would be hard to tell that a tree used to be there. The problem with this strategy was that it will only last for a short while. Sooner or later, the tree would begin to grow again. Yes, the trunk, the branches and the leaves would all grow back and I would be faced with the same dilemma as in the beginning. A second option would be to pull the tree up by the roots. Yes, there would be a hole left there, which I would have to fill in with dirt or another plant, but one thing is for sure, that tree that I pulled up would never grow back again. This has to be our motive for engaging in spiritual warfare; to bind things in the spirit so that they will become extinct forever. We then can release things in the spirit so that their manifestation is assured and we will have the complete victory.

SATAN'S KINGDOM HIERARCHY

Satan has a well organized and systematic kingdom. While the Church argues over doctrine, church policy, who has the largest church, and who puts on the grandest church "show", the Devil is very focused on his mission of wiping the Church out. By wiping the Church out, Satan will be able to keep his position as the god of this world. In **2 Corinthians 4:4** Paul states *"In whom the god of this world hath blinded the minds of them which believe not..."* Satan is allowed to be the god of this world because of man's lack of consciousness concerning his power through God. When man is outside of the merciful relationship with the true and living God, the god of this world is able to blind his eyes, leaving him in confusion, weakness, and unable to navigate

[113]

through life in victory.

Satan wants to control the air waves and the atmosphere. It is not enough for us to pray about things in our personal lives or our local churches. Satan wants to control the air space above your space; he wants it all. This explains Satan's exploitation of television, radio, music, and the Internet. Satan is controlling all of these outlets because the children of God are not warring in the spirit to take back what is rightfully theirs. Paul says in **Ephesians 2:2**, *"Wherein in time past ye walked according to the course of this world, according to the prince of the power of the air, the spirit that now worketh in the children of disobedience"* Paul emphasizes Satan's dominion of the air, which can only be broken by the power of God. Jesus also called Satan the *Prince of this world* in **John 14:30**.

In recent years, the world has seen the rise of terrorism and terrorist groups. These terrorist groups have a very distinct mission and seek to fulfill that purpose on a daily basis. People are killed, buildings are bombed, and people are kidnapped daily because of the *"Jihad"* that these terrorists have waged on the world. Please note that these terrorist groups are just manifestations of the kingdom of Satan which is focused, resolved and determined to block the plan of God for His people. Terrorism is a good example of how Satan operates. He terrorizes, destroys, and wages war in multiple locations, yet all of these acts are connected to one kingdom. Matthew records, *"And Jesus knew their thoughts, and said unto them, Every kingdom divided against itself is brought to desolation; and every city or house divided against itself shall not stand; And if Satan cast out Satan, he is divided against himself; how shall then his kingdom stand?"* **(Matthew 12:25-26).** Therefore, Jesus does not leave us to wonder about whether or not we are fighting an organized foe. Satan is armed and dangerous...how about you?

PRINCIPALITIES

A principality is a chief ruler or being of the highest rank and order in Satan's kingdom. The Greek word is *arche* which means *first.* A principality is a magistrate. A principality is the official entrusted with the administration of the laws of the Devil's kingdom. The like force in God's Kingdom would be an archangel such as Michael. In the book of Daniel, we see that Daniel found himself in a struggle against a principality that was trying to keep the word of God from getting to him. **Daniel 10:13** states, *"But the prince of the kingdom of Persia withstood me one and twenty days: but lo Michael, one of the chief princes, came to help me; and I remained there with the kings of Persia."* In this text, the angel Gabriel was explaining to Daniel that there was a battle taking place. This battle was between Gabriel and a demonic principality over the releasing of Daniel's word from God. Please note that the principality that was opposing Daniel's word was so strong that Gabriel had to get help from Michael, the archangel, in order to release the word of God. Gabriel states that this evil principality withstood him. This was an act of defiance against the designated authority of God. Gabriel was given a responsibility to deliver the Word to Daniel, but was intercepted in the atmosphere. This is why it is very important that we engage in consistent, effectual warfare. These types of principalities will often require a unified effort in the Body of Christ in order to rebuke or bind. This is why Gabriel needed help.

Principalities hover over regions of our world. These are national and territorial spirits whose job is to orchestrate the mass destructions, chaos, and wickedness in those nations and territories. This is why various countries and regions have a theme or identifying characteristic that the people who live there abide by. There are significant consistencies in the way and mode principalities operate in various geographical areas. Areas that are close to or surrounded by water, dry or desert areas, tropical areas, heavily forested, and countless other areas may have consistencies in the way principalities express themselves in government, people and atmosphere. The children of God in those areas must band together in order to bind this type of demonic force. Their hold on the minds of men and systems is so interwoven that only a unified prayer effort will break it. If Christians continue to allow dissemination to keep them from focusing on the importance of unity in spiritual warfare, the enemy will continue to have a chokehold on the lives of men and women who have not experienced the power of the gospel.

POWERS

Powers are authorities that derive their power from and execute the will of the chief rulers or principalities. They are the entities that execute macro-level strongholds, and act as governors and ambassadors under the administration of the principalities. Some traditions say that the fallen angels who broke the heaven/world boundaries by having intercourse with the daughters of men were Powers according to Genesis 6:1-5. Yet, because these spirits didn't have dominion over any territory, they must have been wicked spirits which will be discussed later. Powers have the right (through the authority of the principality) to control and govern areas controlled by the principalities. Powers have dominion over an area or sphere of a jurisdiction. Powers can be likened to a president's cabinet who are all appointed by the president. Each power has a specific purpose that ties into the overall goals and objectives of Satan's kingdom.

RULERS OF DARKNESS

Rulers of Darkness are spirits that seek to manifest themselves in the natural world governments at all levels. World kings, presidents, governors, majors, and other officials, if living in darkness, can fall prey to desires, motives, and goals of Satan's kingdom. The rulers of darkness are the spirits behind many of our world rulers today. These demons provoke leaders to pride, oppressive laws, and anything that is anti-God. These spirits use world rulers to prepare the way for the anti-christ which will be made manifest after the rapture of the Church. These spirits have influenced leaders such as Rameses II, Nebuchadnezzar, Herod, Nero, and Hitler. Currently, these spirits reign heavily in leaders in Middle Eastern countries in the form of violence, world domination desires, human oppression and destructive planning. Mahmoud Ahmandinejad, Kim Jon IL, Vladimir Putin, Omar Balshir, and countless city board members, mayors, governors and federal government officials in the United States have proven to be operating under the influence of a ruler of darkness. In the Western countries, these spirits are expressing themselves in leaders through compromise, deceit, and arrogance. In unindustrialized nations, these spirits manifest themselves through corruptive, money hoarding leaders who allow poverty, disease, bribery and suppression to run rampant in their countries.

SPIRITUAL WICKEDNESS

Spiritual wickedness seek to express their wicked, foul, abominable, and filthy character in the lives of men. These wicked spirits seek to seduce man into disobeying the word of God, commit all manner of evil and destructive acts, tempt, taunt, and irritate the believer, and create confusion and vile expressions in the lives of men. **Matthew 12:43-45** *states, "When the unclean spirit is gone out of a man, he walketh through dry places, seeking rest, and findeth none. Then he saith, I will return into my house from whence I came out; and when he is come, he findeth it* *empty, swept, and garnished. Then goeth he, and taketh with himself seven other spirits more wicked than himself, and they enter in and dwell there: and the last state of that man is worse than the first, Even so shall it be also unto this wicked generation."*

Spiritual wickedness link themselves to people on a personal level. They are the foot soldiers and the grassroots movement of Satan. There are two types of individuals who become conduits of spiritual wickedness. The first type of individual is the incognizant, unspiritual, and unaware. This type also includes those who have no moral center. People who are unaware of the reality of demon spirits are often targets for spiritual wickedness. Even children of God struggle with these spirits. Spiritual wickedness will do anything to access an individual. They will use drugs, media, internet, psychological disabilities, social and emotional traumas, addictions and other ailments and vices to gain access into the lives of unaware individuals. The second type is people who have had their understanding seared by the socialization process of this world through the devil and willingly seek spiritual wickedness as their source of religion and life practice. These people join the occult, humanistic, or Satanist groups and willingly accept doctrines of demons. Examples of spiritual wickedness include spirits of divination, observers of times, enchanters, psychics, consulters, familiar spirits, charmers, sorcerers, mediators, Jezebel spirits, witches, warlocks, imps, strongholds, and generational curses which all fall into this level of evil **(Exodus 7: 11, Deuteronomy 18:10-12, Leviticus**

[119]

19:31, 1 Samuel 28, 2 Kings 9:22, 30; Jeremiah 27: 9, Revelation 2:20). Most people are dealing with this level of demon.

Spiritual wickedness is one of the lowest levels in Satan's kingdom, but very dangerous. They are the most prevalent, because they keep people tied up in struggles while demonic systems in the upper level ranks become stronger. The only difference between spiritual wickedness and other levels is their realm of systemic influence. These wicked spirits seek to fulfill their lust through the bodies of humans, because they themselves have no ability to be seen, heard, or felt in the natural realm without a human vessel. These are the whispering spirits. These are spirits that provoke thoughts that are ungodly and aid man in fulfilling the lust that he already possesses through the flesh. Spirits of depression, sickness, apathy, suicide, murder, lying, fornication and other such spirits all fall within this category in Satan's kingdom.

An example of this type of demon is also found in **Mark 5:1-13.** The following text documents the intricate operations of this level. I will give explanations after various verses in order to highlight how these wicked demons function and how they must be conquered.

"And they came over unto the other side of the sea, into the country of the Gadarenes.

²*And when he was come out of the ship, immediately there met him out of the tombs a man with an unclean spirit,*

These spirits will always keep people around dead things. One of the identifying characteristics of spiritual wickedness is their influence on people to embrace and connect with dead things. People will engage in drugs, abusive relationships, evil music and entertainment, ungodly people and unproductive behaviors when spiritual wickedness has attached to them. Note that the man in the text came out of the tombs. He was around filthy, decomposing bodies daily.

³*Who had his dwelling among the tombs; and no man could bind him, no, not with chains: ⁴Because that he had been often bound with fetters and chains, and the chains had been plucked asunder by him, and the fetters broken in pieces: neither could any man tame him.*

Note that no one could bind this man because of the strength of the demon. Nothing natural can defeat spiritual wickedness. There are no laws man can pass, secular educational curriculum, or humanistic philosophies that can restrict a demon spirit from expressing its lust. The people in this text tried to bind the man with chains, but the man broke them every time. People bound by spiritual wickedness cannot control their behaviors and cannot be controlled by man's systems. Man is no match for spiritual wickedness without the power of God.

⁵*And always, night and day, he was in the mountains, and in the tombs, crying, and cutting himself with stones.*

This demon caused the man to live away from his family and society. Spiritual wickedness will cause people to be withdrawn, to hurt themselves, and to experience extreme emotional, physical and spiritual pain. Note that the man couldn't get any rest. It is the job of spiritual wickedness to keep man on a rollercoaster of extremes. One moment the man was sleeping, but the next moment he was awake crying. One moment the man was safe, but the next moment he was trying to kill himself. This is the spirit that plagues many young people. The music, pop-culture, and trends of this generation are influenced by spiritual wickedness. These spirits attach themselves to young people in an attempt to abort the next generation of Kingdom kids.

6But when he saw Jesus afar off, he ran and worshipped him,

All demons have to acknowledge and bow down to Jesus. This is why the believer must remain under the covering of Christ.

7And cried with a loud voice, and said, What have I to do with thee, Jesus, thou Son of the most high God? I adjure thee by God, that thou torment me not.

The demon was not aware of the plan of God and the time frame by which judgment on earth would be revealed. He acknowledges Jesus and assumes that He was coming to execute judgment. Demons fear and tremble at the power of Jesus.

⁸For he said unto him, Come out of the man, thou unclean spirit. ⁹And he asked him, What is thy name? And he answered, saying, My name is Legion: for we are many.

Note that Jesus commanded the spirit to come out and then asked its name. When we war with these spirits, we must call them by their name. Whether they are spirits of sickness, poverty, bondage, rebellion or depression, they must be called by their name. This demon reported that his name was Legion. A legion is a military unit. In Rome, these heavy infantries varied in size from hundreds to over 6,000. Thus, this man was not being possessed by one spirit, but an army of demons. These demons often travel in packs and wait for one to gain access into a vessel. When one gets access, it will attempt to allow others into that vessel. Thus, the state of the individual becomes worse as time progresses.

¹⁰And he besought him much that he would not send them away out of the country. ¹¹Now there was there nigh unto the mountains a great herd of swine feeding. ¹²And all the devils besought him, saying, Send us into the swine, that we may enter into them.

As stated before, these spirits desire to express themselves in the natural realm through living things. Thus, they didn't want Jesus to cast them out without giving them another place to reside. As seen in Matthew 12:43-45, these spirits will wander until they find a place to fulfill their filth. These legions begged Jesus to send them into pigs.

[123]

¹³*And forthwith Jesus gave them leave. And the unclean spirits went out, and entered into the swine: and the herd ran violently down a steep place into the sea, (they were about two thousand;) and were choked in the sea."*

As soon as this legion was given permission by Jesus to enter the swine, it immediately killed the whole herd. This is what they ultimately wanted to do to the man they had possessed. Spiritual wickedness will utilize man as a home as long as the initiatives of Satan's kingdom are being fulfilled. When there is no more use for the person, spiritual wickedness will destroy them.

WHAT'S THE POINT?

The purpose of examining and understanding Satan's kingdom structure is not to dazzle you with Satan's organization. Rather, it is to increase your awareness of God's trust in our ability through Him to engage in spiritual warfare. Whether it is a principality, power, ruler of darkness, or spiritual wickedness, Paul makes it emphatically clear that we have been equipped to take up this war. The wrestling that takes place between the believer and the enemy is not a pastime affair done without an end result in mind. God has already secured us the victory through the work of the cross and the power of the Holy Spirit. We then must increase our spirituality and faith in order to defeat the enemy in our lives, communities, churches, and nation. To read Paul's words with natural eyes, one would be intimidated, fearful, or anxious about the plight of man. But when we look at Satan's kingdom through the eyes of God, we will see a defeated foe, only empowered by our lack of spirituality, commitment, and belief. As you grow in God and begin to receive His directions into various battles, you will grow to the place where you will be able to boldly confront and defeat all levels of demonic force through the power of the Holy Ghost.

Discussions, Reflections, and Activities

1. What are the four hierarchal positions in the enemy's kingdom?

2. Choose one of the positions in the enemy's kingdom hierarchy and explain how this level negatively affects the lives of men and women.

3. Make a list of government officials who can be persuaded by a principality and pray for them.

4. The author describes our warfare as being in the "indefinite present". Discuss your thoughts about this statement. What is the lesson learned from this fact concerning warfare?

5. Research: The author discussed "Guerrilla Warfare" in describing the type of warfare the child of God is engaged in. Using the Internet, library, or other qualitative data, research military

and battle tactics. How can this information be used to equip the children of God for **spiritual warfare?**

Notes:

_____

_____

_____

_____

_____

_____

_____

_____

_____

_____

_____

_____

_____

_____

_____

_____

_____

_____

_____

_____

_____

_____

> *"For we wrestle not against flesh and blood, but against principalities, against powers, against the rulers of the darkness of this world, against spiritual wickedness in high places."*

> *Ephesians 6:12*

Chapter 7

UNDERSTANDING AND BREAKING STRONGHOLDS

When you are able to funnel all of your weapons through God, you will be able to participate with other anointed children of God within the Body in "pulling down strongholds". The word stronghold comes from the Greek word **Ochyroma** which means *fortress or prison.* Strongholds can be demonic, worldly, or godly. A demonic stronghold happens when an individual has been directly captured by a demonic spirit and is held to the lust, desires, and

[127]

wickedness of that spirit. The demonic stronghold becomes possession and influence which can become the norm within the possessed individual's life. Often times, this tragedy happens outside of the individual's awareness and consciousness. Worldly strongholds are the most common stronghold among mankind because it is difficult to perceive without the guiding light of the Holy Spirit. Satan uses worldly strongholds as an extension of demonic influences to fulfill his ultimate desire of keeping men captive, bound and oppressed. These strongholds are primarily thoughts and ideas that people allow to become permanent in their minds. Much of recent Christian literature has been created to combat this process from happening and move people to having their minds renewed. The thoughts fueling this world's systems can become a block from people moving into the blessings found in the Kingdom of God. Let's look at some examples in scripture concerning demonic and worldly strongholds.

Matthew 12:28-29, *"And if Satan cast out Satan, he is divided against himself; how shall then his kingdom stand? And if I by Beelzebub cast out devils, by whom do your children cast them out? Therefore they shall be your judges. But if I cast out devils by the Spirit of God, then the Kingdom of God is come unto you. Or else how can one enter into a strong man's house, and spoil his goods, except he first bind the strong man? and then he will spoil his house."*

This is a powerful set of scripture because it brings to light three points concerning warring against strongholds. First, Satan will not cast out Satan. In other words, Satan's kingdom is not divided, but unified. Someone possessing a stronghold cannot break another's stronghold of equal or greater strength. The very suggestion of it is ludicrous and will prove to be nothing more than a lot of bodily exercise and show; none of which is an expression of true authority over the enemy. Many supposed great preachers whip people up into an emotional frenzy, yelling out lots of declaratives concerning the expulsion of Satan out of one's life. But, if they themselves are bound by strongholds, they are not breaking any strongholds.

Secondly, the significant manifestation of the Kingdom of God is the expulsion of Satan's kingdom. If Satan is still in the midst, we know that God is not present, because God's Kingdom will immediately remove Satan's authority in any place at anytime. Jesus said in **Matthew 12:28-29**, *"If I cast out devils by the Spirit of God, then the Kingdom of God is upon you."* The presence of the Kingdom of God will expel the enemy. When we break strongholds, God's Kingdom is then free to take up residence in the vacant area. The believer must then be ready for Satan's revolt attack to try to regain the area now under the control of the Kingdom of God.

Finally, Jesus talks about binding the strong man. There is no need to try to decorate a house if you have not first taken possession of that house. The reason many

Christians live in defeat is because the strongman in their life has not been bound yet. Until it's bound, the believer will continue to live in defeat. It would be like claiming to own a house in which you only are able to experience the bedroom because you have a mad dog running around the rest of the house. Until the mad dog is captured and put out, you will be confined to your room with the door locked. This is the way many live. Demonic and worldly strongholds will restrict the ability and potential of the believer, leaving them unproductive and ineffective in the Kingdom. The following scripture was discussed earlier in the book, but for the sake of this new topic, let's reconsider it.

Matthew 12:43-45 continues this discussion stating, *"When the unclean spirit is gone out of a man, he walketh through dry places, seeking rest, and findeth none. Then he saith, I will return into my house from whence I came out; and when he is come, he findeth it empty, swept, and garnished. Then goeth he, and taketh with himself seven other spirits more wicked than himself, and they enter in and dwell there: and the last state of that man is worse than the first. Even so shall it be also unto this wicked generation."* There is much open to commentary in these passages, but I want you to focus your attention on the reattaching nature of a stronghold. Strongholds can reattach themselves to people. When a demonic spirit is cast out it is unsettled. This is because demon spirits need a body in order to express themselves in the natural realm. Thus, demons will always seek someone to embody in order to fulfill their lust. The house in the text was swept and garnished. The Greek word for garnished is **kosmeo** which means to *put in order, arranged and decorated*. The house had been brought into order, which is something that a stronghold comes to destroy, God's order. Thus, in order to ruin the garnishing of this house, the spirit needed to get seven additional spirits more evil than it.

When a stronghold is broken or cast out, it must be replaced with the Kingdom of God. This replacement includes the infilling of the Holy Spirit. When we war against these evil and vile spirits, we must replace their vacancies with the Holy Spirit, so that they can never return again. Many people have left church meetings feeling refreshed because of the anointing that destroyed a yoke off of their lives. Yet, if they are not filled with the Holy Spirit, they are left open and defenseless against a stronghold returning. Also, if old ideas and thoughts are not replaced with the word of God and new Kingdom principles, the person will be left open and defenseless against a stronghold returning.

In **Judges 6:1-6** the children of Israel found themselves out of the favor of the Lord for seven years. The Bible says in verse 2, *"And the hand of Midian prevailed against Israel: and because of the Midianites the children of Israel made them the dens which are in the mountains, and caves, and strong holds."* The Israelites experienced the devastating effects of living in a stronghold, which was the inability to protect their produce, harvest and resources. Every time they planted food, the Midianites would come in and destroy and steal their food during harvest time. Thus, the Israelites were stuck in this cycle of tilling, planting, cultivating, yet having it destroyed at harvest. This is the way people bond by strongholds live. It is not that they are lazy or not good people. But to live in a stronghold is to live without full utility of one's produce, thus becoming famished. Every time something good happens, a stronghold will be the entity that will destroy it. Either through the expression of dysfunctional behaviors or through the debilitating internal struggles that people contend with; strongholds are a definite enemy in this spiritual war. We must fight against strongholds through the word of God. The child of God cannot engage in warfare while trapped in a stronghold or without addressing the places in our society where strongholds exist.

GODLY STRONGHOLDS

The last type of stronghold is a Godly stronghold. God prepares safe places for His people to be shielded from the enemy and puts them in strategic positions against the tricks of the enemy. A Godly stronghold gives the believer a strategy, protection and an advantage against the enemy. Throughout scripture there are many examples of God placing His people in strategic positions to win battles against the enemy. Let's look at some examples of Godly strongholds.

Job 1:9-10 *"Then Satan answered the LORD, and said, Doth Job fear God for nought? Hast not thou made an hedge about him, and about his house, and about all that he hath* *on every side? thou hast blessed the work of his hands, and his substance is increased in the land. "*

~Please note that because God had a hedge around Job, Satan did not have access to him. This hedge was a Godly stronghold. Only God could give access to Job, which allowed Job to serve the Lord in peace and experience the power of prosperity and favor due all of God's children.

Judges 9: 51-53 *"But there was a strong tower within the city, and thither fled all the men and women, and all they of the city, and shut it to them, and gat them up to the top of the tower. And Abimelech came unto the tower, and fought against it, and went hard unto the door of the tower to burn it with fire. And a certain woman cast a piece of a millstone upon Abimelech's head, and all to break his skull."*

~The people found solitude and safety in the tower. The key is that the woman was put in a strategic position that allowed for her to simply drop a stone down from the tower to kill Abimelech. It didn't matter how strong he was. His strength was no match for her position. When we are in God's stronghold, we are put in strategic positions against the enemy.

1 Samuel 23:14 *"And David abode in the wilderness in strong holds, and remained in a mountain in the wilderness of Ziph. And Saul sought him every day, but God delivered him not into his hand."*

~The dilemma here is that although David could have killed Saul, in order to remain under authority until God's given time, he had to trust in the Lord for safety and refuge. He hid himself in strongholds, caves and holes, in the wilderness to remain safe. While in the stronghold, Saul could not find him. When we place ourselves into God's stronghold, the attacks of the enemy will be futile.

Proverbs 18:10 *"The name of the Lord is a strong tower: the righteous runneth into it, and is safe."*

~The name of God, Jesus, is a strong tower for the believer. It is a safe place that the believer can reside in. The tower is a place of refuge but also a place of war. It gives the believer a strategic place to see the enemy when he is coming and to stop the enemy's attacks. Note that the righteous run into the strong tower. Retreat will sometimes become the only option for the believer who has been warring continually. But we don't retreat as the world does, we retreat or rest, in the safety of our Lord's Name; being revived to go back into the fight. There are times in which the believer will be out in the field fighting and other times in which the best position is from a place of safety.

A stronghold can also be defined as all *philosophy, ideals, ungodly reasoning, and demon inspiration that are anti-God which leads to lifestyles and cultures of ungodliness that are managed, facilitated, and perpetuated by principalities, powers, and spiritual wickedness in high places.* A spirit of poverty, lust, suicide, sickness or any other demonic spirit is an idea harbored by a spirit and therefore must be bound by its root. The root is the idea that the spirit springs forth from. As a believer, you have the power to pull down all strongholds set up by the devil. When we pull down strongholds in the spirit, we will see results in the natural realm. As stated before, we wrestle not against flesh and blood. We must use our weapons to attack and pull down strongholds in the spirit so that we can be productive warriors in the name of our Lord. These stronghold "thoughts" give birth to every wicked, evil, blasphemous and anti-God expression we see in the natural realm. A stronghold weaves itself into the life of an individual, slowly and methodically. **1 Timothy 4:1** states, *"Now the Spirit speaketh expressly, that in the latter times some shall depart from the faith, giving heed to seducing spirits, and doctrines of devils"*. The enemy has injected himself into the airwaves of this information generation and caused many to die through the influence of his ideas and doctrines. Note that the spirits are described in Timothy as seducing. The word seducing used in this verse is a Greek word, *planos*, which means *roving (as a tramp), an impostor or misleader, or deceiver*. Thus, these seducing spirits attempt to mislead and are imposters of the truth. Once accepted, these spirits become strongholds that are difficult to break. This is the reason sound doctrine and correct interpretation of scripture is of the utmost importance.

Strongholds are established by a systematic process; they don't just happen overnight. Beginning as a demonic influenced idea, strongholds evolve in the lives of people to become a fortress that is not easily broken. The end result is built on smaller sequential exposures to the enemy and spiritual failings that ultimately lead to a fortress that is hard to be destroyed. Bishop Alfred Itiowe, an expert in the study of strongholds, has in-depth experience in breaking strongholds off of people's lives through the power of God. In his book, *Subduing Satanic Strongholds,* he writes, *"Internal strongholds are the footholds of the enemy within an individual's life where great havoc is done against his total well being. The biggest and most insignificant footholds that may be unimaginable in terms of size and degree. These insignificant footholds include pride, unforgiving spirit, bitterness, envy and their likes...A little internal stronghold may cause a lot of devastation in lives and lands"*[10] pg. 48.

There are key signs that indicate the presence of a stronghold. One of the signs that a stronghold is prevailing is cycles of ungodly behaviors and situations. When an individual is in a perpetual cycle of ungodly behaviors, it is no doubt the result of a stronghold. Often times the individual will minimize the behaviors by saying, "It's just a habit" or "It's just me, being me" or "I can stop, I just mess up every now and then". These are statements of justifying defeat which is the result of the person feeling helpless. That helplessness is due to the stronghold that has them captive.

Another indicator of a stronghold is the prevalence of spiritually inhibiting cultures and/or lifestyles. Although there are many things present in the world that one could partake in that would not be a sin, there are definitely

---

[10] Itiowe, Alfred. "Subduing Satanic Strongholds". Living Treasures Publications (2003). Enugu State, Nigeria

cultures and lifestyle choices that will lead to sin and an absence of the presence of God in one's life. The reason many find it difficult to change their behavior is because after making a choice to change, they never change their environments or life patterns. If a young man wants to be delivered from promiscuous sex, he must not only have that spirit cast off of him, but he must also change his associates, music choices and clothing styles. All of these factors are indicative of a culture that must be broken if he or she is ever to live free from sexual strongholds and begin engaging in spiritual warfare.

When an individual exhibits an inability to accept the word of God, it is another clear indication that a stronghold is present. Satan hates the word of God and wants men and women to live in rebellion. There is nothing, and I mean nothing, that God hates more than a rebellious spirit. Many pastors experience this from various members of their congregation. As they attempt to teach the word of God without reserve and pure, they may encounter some anger, resentment, and even combativeness from people who claim to be children of God. When an individual refuses to accept the word of God, one of two things is in play. Either they are not a child of God, or they are a child of God who is in bondage to a stronghold. Children of God love the word of God, even when it makes them uncomfortable or reflective of some things that they personally need to change. I have taught seminars in which an individual will become argumentative, wanting me to show them in scripture where the Bible say they can't drink, smoke, party or listen to worldly music. There is a difference between someone wanting clarity and someone who is bound by a stronghold. I immediately enter into prayer for individuals who are unable to receive the word of God, because without the word of God, we cannot be saved.

Another sign of a stronghold is when an individual is unproductive in what are seemingly spiritual things. When an individual does something spiritual like pray, pay tithes or worship, yet doesn't yield any fruit from that engagement, a stronghold is prevalent in some other area of their life. Take tithing for instance. If an individual pays their tithes but steals to get the tithes they pay, they will not experience the benefit of that tithe. If an individual works the altar and is consistent in church attendance, but has a heart of unforgiveness, they will not reap the benefits of their consistency and service at church. Satan loves for children of God to engage in a lot of action in the house of God, yet never receive any results from those actions. The enemy does not want children of God to reap profit from following Kingdom principles, because the lack of results discourages faith and mobility towards God's divine will. Therefore, strongholds have to be broken, so that the other areas in a person's life can be loosened up and flow prosperously.

Generational curses are deadly and very powerful strongholds that must also be broken. A generational curse is when the sins and behaviors that are contrary to the word of God exhibited by one generation are passed down to the next. Alcoholism, ungodly sexual behavior, deceit, murder, and rebellion are all examples of generational curses that can be passed from one generation to the next. A generational curse is not just transferred from one biological generation to the next, but also from one spiritual generation to the next. Some churches have been plagued with multiple ungodly men in charge of them; men of God who were riotous, adulterers, false, mean spirited, predators, or deceitful. This type of stronghold whether in one's biological or spiritual body, begins as a spiritual wickedness until it is woven into upper levels of demonic force, such as a strong principality, which will require a unified effort by believers in order to break.

There are many in the Body of Christ living defeated lives because of the ideas they have embraced that are false, tainted, or against the truth of the word of God. Spirits manifest their anti-God thoughts through the lives of men; entangling man in a demonic social system that can only be unraveled and destroyed by the truth of the word of God. The truth of the gospel is the power of God unto salvation. Not messages of prosperity, church growth, gifts of the spirit, or even church hierarchy have the power to break the hold that the devil has on the lives of men. Only the pure, unadulterated gospel has the power to save men and women, change lives, and give men and women access to eternal life. The good news is that the plan of salvation was prepared before the foundations of the world, scripted in the lives of men, and evolved to a climatic tip with God wrapping Himself in flesh in the person of Jesus Christ our Savior. Jesus lived in a world of

[139]

sin, yet knew no sin, died for sin and condemned sin in the flesh, was crucified for sin, buried for three days, and rose again on the third day with all power in heaven and earth in His hands. He then gave the Comforter (Holy Spirit) to lead and guide believers into all truth while sealing the believer until the day of redemption. It is the mystery of godliness, which is found in the gospel, which furnishes the power of the believer to speak with authority against the wiles of the devil.

In **1 Timothy 3:16** it says, *"And without controversy great is the mystery of godliness (piety, holiness, right standing with God): God was manifest in the flesh, justified in the spirit, seen of angels, preached unto the Gentiles, believed on in the world, received up into glory."* The revelation truth of the gospel is what the devil fights against with all his might, and it is this same truth that has subjected the believer to hope and authority in the spirit. Paul stamps the power of the gospel in Romans when he states, *"For I am not ashamed of the gospel of Christ: for it is the power of God unto salvation to everyone that believeth; to the Jew first, and also to the Greek" (Romans 1:16).* It is the gospel that dispels the myths and anti-God thoughts perpetuated by demonic strongholds; liberating man into the wealth of the Kingdom of God. As truth comes into the lives of men, strongholds must leave. This is why it is imperative that the children of God keep themselves under the unadulterated word of God. It is also important that the believer use the word of God to nullify the strongholds in their life and in the lives of people who would come to know Jesus as their Lord and Savior.

Discussions, Reflections, and Activities

1. Discuss three types of demonic strongholds and explain what people must do to break free and stay free from these strongholds.

2. Discuss four signs that a stronghold is present in someone's life.

3. The author presents strongholds as a demonic bondage that begins as an idea or thought. Use the chart below to explore substitutions for ungodly thoughts and actions. Write the ungodly thought or actions on the left and a godly substitute on the right.

Exchanging Strongholds Chart

Ungodly Stronghold	Exchange For	Godly Actions and Character
Revenge		Forgiveness

	⌐→	
	⌐→	
	⌐→	
	⌐→	

4. Let's get transparent! Discuss with a partner or small group an area in your life where you have struggled or currently struggle. Each partner or group member should have time to share and hear feedback concerning support and potential solutions to the presented issues.

Notes:

_____

_____

_____

_____

_____

_____

"This charge I commit unto thee, son Timothy, according to the prophecies which went before on thee, that thou by them mightiest war a good warfare".

1 Timothy 1:18

←————————————————————————→

Chapter 8

A CONTRAST OF SOLDIERS
"The Good vs. The Bad"

As a believer, you must always be mindful that you are a soldier. Soldiers are prepared for war both mentally and physically. Some would argue that the mental training of a soldier is more important than the physical training. If a soldier is strong mentally, they can endure war, battle, torture and will not be afraid of death. A good soldier always has the battle at forefront of his mind. A perfect example of a good soldier is a man named Uriah. Let's read the story concerning this good soldier. In **2 Samuel 11:1 it** says,

"And it came to pass, after the year was expired, at the time when kings go forth to battle, that David sent Joab, and his servants with him, and all Israel; and they destroyed the children of Ammon, and besieged Rabbath. But David tarried still at Jerusalem."

The first point that I want you to take note of is that a good soldier should always be in the place God has ordained him or her to be in. David, the anointed king of Israel, should have been on his way to battle with the rest of the kings, but instead, he sent Joab. When God has given you a calling and a commission, he expects you to work diligently in the area of your calling. If you are outside of God's divine will, defeat is inevitable. You possess power and anointing only when you are fulfilling the word of God in your life. When we decide to be lazy or apathetic concerning God's commission, we open ourselves up to temptation, ungodly trials, and a compromised testimony.

For example, if God gives you a word of encouragement to communicate to someone and you decide not to give it, please understand that you have taken yourself out of the will of God and are open to the shame of defeat. David's first sin was not committing adultery with Bathsheba, but failing to fulfill his role as an anointed king. Let's continue reading the story. **2 Samuel 11:2-3** says,

"And it came to pass in an eveningtide, that David arose from off his bed, and walked upon the roof of the king's house: and from the roof he saw a woman

washing herself, and the woman was very beautiful to look upon. And David sent and inquired after the woman. And one said, "Is not this Bathsheba, the daughter of Eliam, the wife of Uriah the Hittite?"

In this verse, David is allowing himself to be entangled with the affairs of this life through the lust of the flesh, lust of the eyes, and the pride of life. The Apostle John gives us a very important principle in understanding the way in which the devil gets access into the life of the believer to nullify the purposes of God. John stated, *"For all that is in the world, the lust of the flesh, and the lust of the eyes, and the pride of life, is not of the Father, but is of the world. And the world passeth away, and the lust thereof: but he that doeth the will of God abideth for ever"* **(1 John 2:16-17).** The Bible stated that David saw the woman washing and that she was beautiful to look upon. This was the lust of the eyes and the lust of the flesh. The temptation was accessed through David's eye and connected with the lust that was already in his flesh. No doubt the images of Bathsheba showering turned over and over in his mind as he began to fantasize about being with her. When lust was complete, David began to operate in pride. The spirit of pride is a spirit of entitlement, arrogance, and stubbornness. He knew that she had a husband, but lust found justification through pride. **James 1:15** says, *"Then when lust hath conceived, it bringeth forth sin: and sin, when it is finished, bringeth forth death.*

David was not ignorant of who she was or who she was married to, but he was determined to possess her. Pride and lust entangled within his spirit causing him to turn away from the laws of God to the law of the flesh. **Romans 7:23** states, *"But I see another law in my members, warring against the law of my mind, and bring me into captivity to the law of sin which is in my members."* Instead of David going out to engage in the war that he was called to, he is now engaged in a war within his body. He was in a war with his carnality, which will always end in defeat for the believer if they are not in the will of God. In this text, David is a perfect example of an irresponsible and bad soldier. The consequence of David allowing himself to be entangled with his flesh, rather than the real war, was the impregnation of Bathsheba. Let's continue reading **2 Samuel 11:6-11** to see the attributes of a good soldier.

And David sent to Joab, saying, Send me Uriah the Hittite. And Joab sent Uriah to David. And when Uriah was come unto him, David demanded of him how, Joab did, and how the people did, and how the war prospered. And David said to Uriah, Go down to thy house, and wash thy feet. And Uriah departed out of the king's house, and there followed him a mess of meat from the king. **But Uriah slept at the door of the king's house,** *with all the servants of his lord, and* **went not** *down to his house. And when they had told .David saying, Uriah went not down unto his house, David said unto Uriah, Camest thou not from thy* *journey. Why didst thou not go down unto thine house? And Uriah said unto David, the ark, and Israel, and Judah, abide in tents; and my lord Joab, and the servants of my lord encamped in the open fields; shall I then go into mine house, to eat and to drink, and to lie with my wife? As thou livest, and as thy soul liveth I will not do this thing.*

In an attempt to mask his sinful act, David attempts to persuade Uriah into having intercourse with his wife while the battle was in progress. However, Uriah, being a good soldier, had the battle at the forefront of his mind. If Uriah had intercourse with Bathsheba, everyone would have assumed that the baby she was pregnant with was his. Not even the king of Israel could convince Uriah to entangle himself with the affections of this life during the battle. Uriah makes an interesting statement in **2 Samuel 11:11**. He questions how one can enjoy the pleasures of this life while other saints are in the battle. Uriah was a real soldier who was determined to keep the mindset, demeanor, and character of a soldier, even if it meant falling out of favor with King David. Uriah remained focused on his commission and position.

Reader, how can you remain idle while the children of God all over the world are in the heat of the battle? How can you watch television while your brothers or sisters are fighting by themselves? You must understand that you are a part of a body. Someone who needs your prayer to stop a fiery dart from hitting them will be hit and wounded because you were not at your battle station. How would you feel if in the heat of battle your battle partner retreated, leaving you surrounded? Reader, if you fall into the category of a bad soldier, you need to ask God to show you those things that are hindering your ability to engage in spiritual warfare. When he does, separate yourself from them. Then after you untangle yourself, get equipped to engage in the battle at hand.

David's lack of focus is an example for all of us who God has called to do great works. It is important that we constantly remind ourselves of what we have been called to and what our purpose is. Paul admonishes his son in the gospel Timothy to stay focused. In **1 Timothy 1:18** Paul states, *"This charge I commit unto thee, son Timothy, according to the prophecies which went before on thee, that thou by them mightiest war a good warfare"*. If David would have remembered the prophecy and covenant given to him from the beginning, he would have been able to fight off the temptation of the devil. If David would have been mindful of the mantle that was on his life, walking in the shadow of Christ who would come as the King of Kings, he would have went to battle with the rest of Israel. Timothy is admonished to remember the prophecy he was given so that he can engage in a good warfare. Not just warfare, but a "good" warfare. I want to be found warring on behalf of the Kingdom of God. The prophecies and callings of God are established by God and are the means by which we have the faith to do great things for Him.

THE CHARACTER OF THE SOLDIER

The character of the soldier is the foundation by which we become tools that create effective spiritual warfare become. Without character, the child of God will only be able to win a few battles before losing the ultimate war. It is awesome to want to make the weapons for spiritual warfare, but if character is not built, the whole war will be lost due to the child of God's inability to endure the sporadic stages that wars entail. In the book of Galatians, Paul outlines what he calls the Fruit of the Spirit. The Fruit of the Spirit is the character quality that God wants all of His children to produce which gives substance, strength, and power to the war that must be waged.

John L. Mastrogiovanni confronts the issue of defiance in the Church in his book, *The Spirit of the Scorpion.* He points out the importance of character in the life of the believer who would want to do anything for God. His premise is that the modern day Church is full of gifted people who have not learned through the spirit of God how to be disciplined, humbled and submissive to authority, thereby causing the collapse of effective ministry. He states, *"In the early church, before the New Testament was ever canonized, they still had to live a life with God's character, or in other words, bear the fruit of the Spirit. Even the church at Corinth, which functioned in the manifestations and expressions of the Holy Spirit, was exhorted to go on with God by a more excellent way".* He continues saying, *"Character doesn't come easy and it doesn't come by correct theology or spiritual*

[150]

manifestations. If it did, the church of Corinth would have been a spiritual giant! But instead they had division, strife, sexual sin, and self-appointed apostles" [11]*pg. 7.*

Consider the statements of Mastrogiovanni. With all of the spiritual gifting the church at Corinth had, they were highly ineffective because they lacked the character of God. Satan knows that our gifts will be null and void if we allow ourselves to slip into a quandary of character flaws. We will continue to make great declarations of faith that won't ever be fulfilled because of the character issues that block God from moving as the Lord of Hosts. David was king, strong, good looking, a psalmist, and articulate. He was wise, creative, a warrior, an investor, and beloved of God, but none of those qualities meant anything in light of his poor character. He still failed with God and therefore, failed in truth. Your very presence at the battle can get you victory when the Lord is on the inside of you, fighting through you.

Paul states, *"But the fruit of the Spirit is love, joy, peace, longsuffering, gentleness, goodness, faith, Meekness, temperance: against such there is no law,"* **(Galatians 5:22-23).** At first glance it would seem that these virtues have very little to do with engaging in warfare. The reality is that these virtues are the premise by which all children of God must conduct their lives and spiritual warfare. When I act out of love, my motives will be pure and clear. David acted out of lust, which clouded his moral vision. When I act out

---

[11] Mastrogiovanni, John L. "The Spirit of the Scorpion-Conquering the Powers of Insurrection. Morris Publishing (1992). Monrovia, CA

[151]

of a spirit of longsuffering, I am able to endure hardship and struggle without complaining or feeling incomplete. When I act out of temperance, I won't make rash or irrational decisions; I will be moderate in both behavior and attitude. Trying to conduct warfare without the character of God is like a bird trying to fly without feathers. The devil gains the advantage when we don't have spirits that bear fruit. The enemy can use our lack of character against us. Through our flawed character, Satan can dismantle our testimony and cause us to be ineffective in ministry due to a loss of credibility among people in and outside of the Church. Therefore, we must seek the character of God so that we can be good soldiers in Our Warfare.

Discussions, Reflections, Activities

1. Based on this chapter, what are the characteristics of a good soldier? What are the characteristics of a bad soldier?

2. Explore partnerships that you, your group, or church can establish with other "good" soldier groups in order to execute a spiritual or social change in your local and regional communities, and in your nation.

3. Describe a time in which you were distracted from completing a task. What caused the distraction? What were the negative consequences?

4. Explore your life commitments. Explore three things

you are committed and loyal to. How do you show your loyalty? What do you do in order to protect those commitments?

5. The author discusses the Fruit of the Spirit as the base foundation of the character of the child of God. Use the chart below to explore your own personal qualities. The chart has the quality/virtue and the Greek word and definition. Mark a **(H)** by qualities you Have, a **(NM)** by qualities you Need More of, and a **(N)** by qualities you Need.

Fruit/Quality	Definition	H, N, NM
Love	(Greek word: *Agape*) Divine love, a strong, ardent, tender, compassionate, devotional to the well being of someone.	
Joy	(Greek word: *Chara*) The emotional excitement, gladness, delight over blessings received or expected for self and for others.	

Peace	(Greek word: *Eirene*) The state of quietness, rest repose, harmony, order, security in the mist of turmoil.
Longsuffering	(Greek word: *Makrothumia*), Patient endurance; to bear long with the frailties, offences, injuries, and provocations of others, without murmuring, repining, or resentment.
Gentleness	(Greek word: *Chrestotes*). A disposition to be gentle, soft-spoken, kind, even-tempered, cultured, and refined in character and conduct.
Goodness	(Greek word: *Agathosune*) The state of being good, kind, virtuous, benevolent, generous, and God-like in life and conduct.
Faith	(Greek word: *Pistis*) The living, divinely implanted, acquired, and created principle of inward and wholehearted confidence, assurance, trust, and reliance in God and all that He says.

Meekness	(Greek word: *Praotes*). The disposition to be gentle, kind, indulgent, even balanced in tempers and passions, and patient in suffering injuries without feeling a spirit of revenge.	
Temperance	(Greek word: *Enkrateia*) Self control; a moderation in the indulgence of the appetites and passions.	
Total: Give 3 points for H, 2pts for NM, and 1pts for N. **Scores: 23-27 Strong, 17-22 Good, 9-16 Weak.**		**Total**

Commentary

Very few people will score in the upper levels of strong. Most children of God must admit that they need more of God's character expressed in their lives.

a. Discuss and/or reflect on the findings of this activity.

Notes:

_____

_____

_____

_____

_____

_____

_____

"Wherefore take unto you the whole armor of God, that ye may be able to withstand in the evil day, and having done all, to stand."

Ephesians 6:13

Chapter 9

THE WHOLE ARMOR OF GOD

Part 1

THE BELT, BREASTPLATE, SHOES AND SHIELD

As stated before, the weapons of our warfare are not to be used in carnal affairs, but for spiritual combat. All entities in the natural realm have foundations that exist in the spiritual realm. Therefore, by warring in the spirit we are able to deal with the foundations of problems which will give us complete victory. Let's read **2 Corinthians 10:4-6** again beginning at verse 4, *"For the weapons of our warfare are not carnal, but mighty through*

[157]

God to the pulling down of strong holds."

Please note that the weapons that we use are not of the flesh. Physical acts have no bearing at all on the spiritual realm. Only actions in the natural that are born out of the will of God through faith will have power in the natural realm. Sometimes we think that because we yell or make a lot of noise in church, that we are affecting events in the spiritual realm. This is not so. Church attendance, participation in church activities, and charitable deeds do not give you power in the spirit. All of these acts are good, but have no direct bearing on being effective in spiritual warfare. No matter how much noise we make at church, what we wear to church, or do in accordance with our religious ideals, none of it gains us the victory in and of itself. You must always understand that the devil is not scared of anything born out of the flesh, because the flesh is the partner of Satan, working to block the plan of God for His people.

Our weapons are "mighty through God". All weapons must be used according to the will of God. God's design, purpose and word are the encasement for His will. There is a lot of disorder in the Body of Christ because some have believed, in err, that they can manage the gifts that God has given them and use them however they want. If God has gifted you with a beautiful voice, that gift is only "mighty" when it is used "through God". If you have the anointing to preach and understand scripture, you are only "mighty" when that anointing is used through God. Many preachers use the gift of persuasion that God has given them to raise money, create division, and belittle people of different belief systems. Yet, the power of preaching is not in how eloquent or articulate one is as a speaker, but one's ability to use that gift through God to affect positive change in the lives of men that will lead them to accepting the gospel.

In **2 Corinthians 10:5** Paul states, *"Casting down imaginations, and every high thing that exalteth itself against the knowledge of God, and bringing into captivity every thought to the obedience of Christ"*. Notice that as believers, our weapons "cast down" imaginations. The assurance that is spoken of in this passage is that there is no knowledge that can stand in the light of God's word. The children of God have the power to cast down imaginations. Imaginations can be used by God to do miraculous things in the Kingdom, but if influenced by the devil, an imagination can lead people to live a life that is anti-God. When Satan is in the mix, the imagination of man is only the expressed thoughts of demonic influences. These demonic imaginations seek for new and creative ways to break the laws and principles of God. Satan hates the laws of God and uses imaginations to seduce man into living in error and a state of moral conflict. It is the imagination that has led us as humankind to actions that are contrary to the will of God throughout all of our history. All throughout the word of God, man has struggled with his imagination. In **Genesis 6:5**, Moses expresses God's dilemma with man, saying, *"And God saw that the wickedness of man was great in the earth, and that every* *imagination of the thoughts of his heart was only evil continually."* From the very beginning, man was not able to bring his mind under subjection to the will of God. That is to say, man has struggled and failed to block demonic influences on his thought processes. These demonic influences only desire to destroy man before he ever receives the truth of the gospel.

Demonic spirits influence high school students to shoot their fellow classmates, people to commit suicide and adults to molest children. It is these demonic thoughts and imaginations that cause racism, murder, and every type of vicious crime known to man. Have you ever noticed that crimes continue to get worse and worse? It is because these demonic ideals are being allowed to run rampant in the spiritual realm and be expressed through the lives of man. The inactivity of the children of God allows the imaginations of man to run wild. We have the power to bring all thoughts into the subjection of Christ. All things should be made to come under subjection to the word of God and His plan. Therefore, we must bind anything that tries to exist outside of the will of God.

In **2 Corinthians 10: 6,** continues, saying, *"And having in a readiness to revenge all disobedience, when your obedience is fulfilled."* As a believer, you have power to pull down the strongholds of sickness, anxiety, depression, rebellion, unbelief, fear, doubt, loneliness, lust, low self-esteem, insecurity, witchcraft and any other strong hold that tries to uplift its ugly head. But note in this passage that Paul stated that the believer should be ready to "revenge" all disobedience. How does the believer revenge disobedience? Do we act as the Angel of the Lord and hurt people who hurt others, kill people who kill others, or steal from people who steal? God forbid. We revenge disobedience by our obedience to the will of God and by warring in the spirit. When Satan steals someone's mind, we preach the gospel with all the more fervency to bring two more people into the Kingdom. When Satan brings sickness into the life of someone, we bind the spirit sickness and speak healing into the situation so that the person leaves that circumstance with a testimony that God is the God that heals. We take our revenge in the spirit, which will result in natural success. We also take revenge by the way we live. We become even more steadfast in faith and the commandments of God, so that we are never used to bring a reproach on the Kingdom of God. We walk holy and upright before the Lord with all of our heart and mind. When people see our love for one another and for God, they will be open to receive the gospel.

Yet, we cannot war in this dimension until our "obedience is fulfilled". Paul does not condone the false ideal that children of God have unlimited access to the power of God without following the rules of the Kingdom. Obedience must always precede spiritual warfare. Remember Uriah, he was a faithful soldier in good standing in the kingdom. Likewise, we must walk in the light and in the spirit of holiness if we want to have power with God. There are many great orators that have bewitched thousands of people into thinking that they have power with God. When in reality, all they have is great speaking ability and a zeal to arouse the emotions of people. If the individual is living unholy, they have nothing more than a form of godliness that denies the power thereof. Therefore, we revenge disobedience by working to nullify disobedience in our own lives. We must stay before God, asking Him to continually help us overcome our deficits, so that we can war on His behalf triumphantly. When we rely on God's holiness, we access the true power that is given to us as believers.

Paul warns Timothy concerning men who have fallen away saying, *"Having a form of godliness, but denying the power thereof: from such turn away. For of this sort are they which creep into houses, and lead captive silly women laden with sins, led away with divers lust, ever learning, and never able to come to the knowledge of the truth"* **(2 Timothy 3:5-7)**. Believers, preachers and biblical scholars all over the world are imitating the anointing of God, but are unwilling to come under subjection to the true authority of God, which requires absolute obedience to His will and word in order to engage in spiritual warfare. Some "leaders" are leading masses of people astray. Making people believe that they are saved and moving in the things of God, when in actuality they are moving on their own strength and emotions; trying to do a spiritual thing through the flesh. We must walk according to the word of God, so that our obedience is fulfilled. Then the covenant blessings can be released to us and we can begin to wage war against the devil and his kingdom. Leaders who lie to their people, making them believe that they can live outside of the laws and precepts of God and do great exploits for God, will be held accountable in the judgment. Dearly beloved, your obedience undergirds your authority to pull down strongholds.

The Bible commands us to put on the whole armor of God. Paul admonishes the Ephesian church in **Ephesians 6:13** saying, *"Wherefore take unto you the whole armor of God, that ye may be able to withstand in the evil day, and having done all, to stand."* Please understand that the whole armor has at least three basic truths about it that you must understand in order to apply this revelation appropriately. In order to prosper in this knowledge, these three areas of truth must first be understood.

The first truth you must internalize is that you must take all of the armor. Not part of the armor or a few pieces, but all of the armor. Beloved, if you don't take the "whole" armor, you put yourself in danger when engaging in spiritual warfare. For example, in 2007, the United States military submitted a report to the President concerning the battle equipment the armed forces were using in Iraq and other nations around the world. The military generals strongly encouraged the administration to release the funding for adequate equipment for the soldiers. Without full supply of weaponry and equipment, the military, as great as it is, would be doomed to suffer great casualties. The believer is the same. If we don't take the whole armor of

God with us into battle, we will suffer great casualties in different areas of our lives and risk losing many battles ahead.

Next, we must understand that the whole armor of God is largely for defense purposes. There is only one piece of equipment that can be used directly as an attack weapon. When we engage in this type of warfare, we are defending what God has already given us through the spirit. Peter writes, *"According as his divine power hath given unto us all things that pertain unto life and godliness, through the knowledge of him that hath called us to glory and virtue"* (2 Peter 1:3). God has given us everything we need to live a productive, powerful life, but we must protect it from the enemy's attacks. This is why Paul tells us to stand. Don't run at the enemy, just stand. Reader, you can engage in full fledge battle while standing in one place. Your sword, which I will speak about later, has the power to go wherever you need it to in order to fight the enemy. But, you cannot fight the devil without first taking a stand.

We live in a world that is fashion and fad driven. One day we are excited about a particular style and the next season we are not. All it takes is a 30 second news report about a negative issue, and most people fall into a spirit of nervousness and anxiety. As the year 2000 approached, because of the fear of computers crashing and expected end time chaos, people went out and stocked up on water, made underground bunkers, and some even sold all their possessions in expectation of the end to come. All of them were wrong. Believer, we are not like the world, being tossed to and fro with every wind of doctrine or idea. We should be solid in our beliefs and therefore able to make a stand in God against the wiles of the devil. Paul says in **Ephesians 4:14**, *"That we henceforth be no more children, tossed to and fro, and carried about with every wind of doctrine, by the sleight of men, and cunning craftiness, whereby they lie in wait to deceive."* Believer, we have to take a stand! We must use the armor to defend the beliefs and blessings we have received in God. Children of God pray for God to work things out for them, but never want to take a stand. Believer, please make no mistake, you will have to take a stand if you want to be victorious in spiritual warfare.

We must also understand that the focus of the armor is on a forward progression. It would even seem that there is no armor for our back in Paul's description. All the armor gives defense to the front of our body. The breastplates in Roman times did give some protection to the back, being a two part overlay protecting the front and the back. Yet, the protection of the breastplate to the back is clearly a protection one would hope not to have to use. If we meet the enemy head on, we will not need to use the back portion of the breastplate. It is of utmost danger to be in a position where you need to use the back plate for protection. This means that if we turn our backs to the enemy in retreat, our spinal cord will be exposed. The spinal cord carries all the neural connections to the rest of the body. Individuals, who have had accidents which caused paralysis, experience the lack of sensation and control of a large portion of their body. If the spinal cord is damaged, the whole body will suffer. Therefore, we cannot turn our backs on the devil.

Another revelation concerning the "exposed" back, is that by doing so, we can remove ourselves out of the covenant blessings of God. Turning back is the same as retreating, returning to former things, and giving up. Turning my back on the devil is dangerous, but going back to the things in my former life or the world is just as dangerous. Either way, I risk losing the battle. Lot's wife looked back and suffered the consequences of such an action. *"But his wife looked back from behind him, and she became a pillar of salt"* **(Genesis 19:26).** We are delivered to be delivered and must therefore stand in that deliverance. Lot's wife didn't realize that the Lord was blessing her with an everlasting deliverance of which she could not turn back from. She was seduced by her lust for the world to look back. Sometimes, we as believers can get fatigued with the spiritual warfare we are engaged in and be tempted to turn back to our former lust and desires which are contrary to the will of God. This turning back will absolutely destroy the victory that you should walk in as a believer.

In **Luke 9:62,** Jesus says, *"No man, having put his hand to the plow, and looking back, is fit for the Kingdom of God."* Many believers are not fit for the Kingdom of God because they refuse to make a stand and not turn back while in the battle. Not only will God not honor such a believer, but the devil will also recognize this deficit and run amuck in the life of that believer. We deceive ourselves when we think that we can hide our deficits, weaknesses, and lack of commitment to God. God is aware of everything in our life and will only respond to faith. The devil is also aware of weaknesses in our lives. The devil can smell blood, sense defeat, and taste unbelief. This is why Peter says, *"Wherefore the rather, brethren, give* **diligence** *to make your* **calling** *and* **election** **sure:** *for if ye do these things, ye shall* **never fall"** (2 Peter 1:10).

THE BELT OF TRUTH

Ephesians 6:14 reads as follows: *"Stand therefore, having your loins girt about with truth, and having on the breastplate of righteousness"*. Notice the first word of this verse, 'Stand"! Don't go back, or step to the side, but *"be strong in the Lord, and in the power of his might"* **(Ephesians 6:10)**. We must stand strong, not feeble and weak kneed, but sturdy and confident. Paul goes on to say that we should have our loins gird with truth. The loin is the area of reproduction and appetite. It is the area between the lower rib and the pelvic area, and is used as a euphemism for the human genitalia. Our ability to multiply, be fruitful and bring forth the ministries and gifts God has planted within our spirits is channeled through our loins. Our appetites for good and evil also lie within the loin area. Believer, you must be able to control ungodly appetites and develop an appetite for the things of God. The loin is the abode of strength and the centerpiece of fruitfulness. Our ability to

[167]

reproduce and be effective is a vital quality that all children of God must have.   An unproductive or ineffective believer is useless to the Kingdom, and God finds no pleasure in him.

Throughout the Bible we see countless examples of the importance of the loins and the ability to produce.   In scripture, the natural examples are women who desire above all in life to have a child. The importance of being able to produce as a symbol of purpose and destiny is shown over and over again. Leah and Rachel desired to produce a child (Genesis 29:31-35, 30:1-24). Tamar received seed from her father-in-law Judah (Genesis 38) in order to produce a child. These examples show the desperation of people in scripture to be productive. David also understood the importance of the loins. On the day of Pentecost, Peter preached to the Jews concerning the foresight of David as it pertains to his seed saying, *"Therefore being a prophet, and knowing that God had sworn with an oath to him, that of the fruit of his loins, according to the flesh, he would raise up Christ to sit on his throne"* **(Acts 2:30)**.   Note that David understood that it wasn't the battles he had won, the treasures he had, nor the reputation he had around the world that made him successful, but rather, the product of his seed (Jesus Christ) which would ultimately define him as one of the greatest kings to ever reign.   Thus, the loin area is symbolic of our ability to be effective.

[168]

Jesus says in **Matthew 5:13**, *"Ye are the salt of the earth: but if the salt have lost his savour, wherewith shall it be salted? It is thenceforth good for nothing, but to be cast out, and to be trodden under foot of men."* Salt is supposed to change the food that it is used in.   In ancient Israel it was used to strengthen the skin of newborn babies. Jesus talks about salt losing its savour, which is its flavor, taste and fragrance.   Salt has integrity.   It changes the things that it is exposed to, yet it is never changed. When you put salt on a steak, the salt doesn't become "steaky", but the steak becomes salty. Just as salt is potent, productive, and effective, the child of God must also be effective.

Because of the importance of the loin area, we must protect it with truth. Not sincerity or honesty (which are positive virtues to possess), but the truth as it pertains to knowledge, revelation and doctrine. Sound doctrine must cover your loins or you will bring forth something that is not of God. **Galatians 1:6** says, *"I marvel that ye are so soon removed from him that called you into the grace of Christ unto another gospel".*   Allowing false information to gird your loins can produce a huge amount of problems for you. You will begin to produce things that are not of God. Anything that is not of God will ultimately become stumbling blocks and hardships in your life. Abraham confronted this problem in Genesis 16 and 21. Rather than standing on the word of God and waiting patiently for his wife Sarah to bear a son, Abraham, at his

[169]

wife's advice, decided to raise up seed through Hagar his maidservant. Abraham eventually had to send Hagar and his son Ishmael away after Ishmael mocked Isaac, the heir to the covenant blessings given to Abraham. Ishmael mocking Isaac is exactly what happens when we produce something that is not in the perfect will of God. Anything that is produced outside of truth will always come back to mock and stifle us from our destiny.

When the loin is not girded with truth, they will be used for the world and not for God. Just as the loin is designed for production, they can also be used for sexual immorality and lasciviousness. Sexual immorality is the seed of unproductiveness and confusion. Many people use their bodies for pleasure and not for godly purposes which is not only detrimental to them, but society as a whole. Teenage pregnancy has resulted in the birth of improperly parented children which has led to deviant behavior among children. Promiscuity has led to the continued increase of sexually transmitted diseases such as HIV and AIDS, gonorrhea, chlamydia, and hepatitis. Uncovered loins have led many to a dysfunctional emotional and social state which has led to the inability of people to gain, develop, and maintain healthy long-term intimate relationships. Consequently, even in the house of God, people are using their bodies as a weapon of war and not of worship. No wonder Paul says to the Corinthian church, *"What? know ye not that your body is the temple of the Holy Ghost which is in you, which ye have of God, and ye are not your own?"* (1 Corinthians 6:19).

The Lord killed Onan for using his body for pleasure and not for purpose. The Bible says, *"And Onan knew that the seed should not be his; and it came to pass, when he went into unto his brother's wife, that he spilled it on the ground, lest that he should give seed to his brother"* **(Genesis 38:9).** Christians today are doing the same thing that Onan did. They want the pleasures of being saved, but don't want to walk in purpose. They want to enjoy the joy of the Lord, the covenant blessings, and the favor that God gives to all His children, but do not want to control themselves and be subject to the will of God. Believer, we must gird our loins with truth and walk therein. When my loin area is covered with truth I will be effective in spiritual warfare. Bible study, Sunday school and other teaching forums must become a priority in your life. You need the word. I need the word. We need the word. The word of God, taught in truth, will provide us with the covering we need in order to be productive, control ungodly appetites, and gain an appetite for things that please God. This is true warfare.

THE BREASTPLATE OF RIGHTEOUSNESS

Next, Paul says we must put on the breastplate of righteousness. Righteousness in this text is holiness, right standing and purity. It is important to note that the righteousness of the breastplate begins in an abstract level of righteousness before developing into more practical and experiential righteousness. The Bible says in **Isaiah 64:6,** *"But we are all as an unclean thing, and all our righteousness are as filthy rags..."* We don't have any righteousness within ourselves. One of the major problems in some Christian denominations is that they have accepted the false idea that we as humans have something pure within ourselves that makes us worthy of the blessings, privileges, and mercies that God has given us. When the Bible speaks of righteousness, it is always connected back to the righteousness of God. Whatever appearance of righteousness we have, it is only the byproduct of the grace of God and a relationship with Him. Therefore, we must have God's righteousness as our breastplate. Notice that the breastplate covers all of your vital organs. Your heart, liver, spinal cord and lungs are all protected by righteousness of Christ Jesus.

The righteousness spoken of in this sense finds its meaning in the Greek word *dikaiosyna-a state of a man who is as he ought to be, righteous, the condition acceptable to God.* This is why God's righteousness must protect our vital organs. It is our right standing with God that gives us victory. There is much deception among Christians concerning what true righteousness is. The deceptive idea that righteousness is found in the natural strength of the believer is dangerous and against the provision of grace by our Lord and Savior Jesus Christ. This deception has kept many from taking up the fight against the kingdom of Satan; lying dormant in guilt, depression and sterility. God gave Abraham a promise that all nations would be blessed through him (I will touch on this subject in the next section). This promise was magnificent and secured through the divine sovereignty of

God, but had to be actualized through the faith of Abraham. The Bible says, *"And he brought him forth abroad, and said, Look now toward heaven, and tell the stars, if thou be able to number them: and he said unto him, So shall thy seed be. And he believed in the LORD; and he counted it to him for righteousness. And he said unto him, I am the LORD that brought thee out of Ur of the Chaldees, to give thee this land to inherit it"* (Genesis 15:5-7). It was not the goodness, prestige, or skill of Abraham that caused him to be blessed by God. Rather, it was his ability to simply believe the word of God. God counted Abraham's belief for righteousness. In other words, God received Abraham's belief and gave him righteousness in return. God will express His righteousness through you as you yield to Him. This is a revelation that Satan hates. Satan wants mankind to try to cover itself with its own righteousness. Satan wants man to try to operate in his own strength, which will leave him prey to the all out attacks of the enemy.

Adam and Eve encountered this problem after their fall. The Bible says, *"And the eyes of them both were opened, and they knew that they were naked; and they sewed fig leaves together, and made themselves aprons"* (Genesis 3:7). Their first inclination after becoming aware of their sin and shame was to try to cover it with fig leaves. They used something from the earth, which was going to be cursed, to cover their shame. Man will always try to find ways to make himself righteous through his own actions. Yet, God, in His mercy and compassion, doesn't allow Adam and Eve to be covered in their own strength. In **Genesis 3:21**, *"Unto Adam* *also and to his wife did the LORD God make coats of skins, and clothed them"*. God covers His people the right way. God covered Adam and Eve with bloody skins, which was a type of Christ who would ultimately come to cover and cleanse all of the world's sin and shame.

Thus, our capacity to breathe the spirit of God throughout our system is based on our ability to protect our lungs. Our heart's strength to pump the blood of Christ throughout our body, allowing healing, life and vitality to reach our complete being, is based on us protecting our chest area. Our ability to have a backbone that strengthens us to stand strong in the midst of trials and tribulations is due to the righteousness of God. It is God's righteousness that protects us from being destroyed by the attacks and lies of the enemy. The enemy will accuse the children of God and cause them to lose their passion and desire to do the will of God. But when we depend wholly on the righteousness of God, we can remain in good standing with Him and continue fighting the good fight of faith.

THE FEET COVERED WITH THE GOSPEL OF PEACE

"And your feet shod with the preparation of the gospel of peace" (Ephesians 6:15)

Your feet should be bound and wrapped with the preparation of the gospel of peace. Roman soldiers would wear foot gear that covered the front of their foot and shin. It also had sharp edges on the heel that would allow them to dig into the dirt when they wanted and needed extra fortification. It is the gospel of peace that fortifies us as believers. The gospel allows us to be firm in our convictions and stand in the freedom and liberty of the New Covenant. Also, note that the covering is for the feet which represent the ability to move when needed. In the context of this text, the key is to stand, but if needed, we have the power to move under the authority of God. But the larger question is, "what is the gospel?"

Most of the time when Christians talk about the gospel, they refer to it as the birth, life, suffering, death, burial, resurrection and ascension of Jesus Christ, and giving of the Holy Spirit which seals our salvation as believers. This description of the gospel is true and accurate in the specific framework of a time and place in history when these culminating events took place to secure salvation for all who would believe. Yet, the gospel should also be seen in a broader context. The gospel is the plan of God to redeem man unto Himself. The gospel plan didn't begin when God hid himself in the womb of Mary, but it is the plan by which all of God's dealings with man have been governed by.

Galatians 3:8 says, *"And the scripture, foreseeing that God would justify the heathen* *through faith, preached before the gospel unto Abraham, saying, In thee shall all nations be blessed.*" Note that Paul is saying that the gospel was preached to Abraham when God gave him the promise of a redeemed seed. Therefore, the cross was the culmination of the plan of God which He had designed from the beginning. Paul says in **Hebrews 4:2**, *"For unto us was the gospel preached, as well as unto them: but the word preached did not profit them, not being mixed with faith in them that heard it."* The children of Israel didn't realize that when God gave them a promise of a land flowing with milk and honey, that this promise was a shadow of the ultimate salvation that He would give to everyone who would believe in Him regardless of gender, ethnicity, or nationality. Yet, because the children of Israel didn't have faith in "the gospel", they couldn't access the promises of God. Therefore, it is faith in God's divine plan of redemption which strikes a death blow to the kingdom of Satan.

God is the author of the gospel, the builder of the plan, and the fulfiller of its provisions. He wrote the plan in eternity, knowing that His creation would fail Him and need to be redeemed and reconciled back to Him. He built the plan from Adam to Mary through His dealings with man and His chosen people; giving us only shadows, types and prophecies of the fulfillment of His plan which was to come. Then He fulfilled the Gospel by wrapping Himself in flesh in the embodiment of Jesus Christ; becoming the propitiation for sin necessary to complete the process of redemption. This is why Paul wrote, *"Now therefore ye are no more strangers and foreigners, but fellow-citizens with the saints, and of the household of God; And are built upon the foundation of the apostles and prophets, Jesus Christ himself being the chief corner stone"* **(Ephesians 2:19-20).** The gospel is God's plan to secure His household of pure worshippers for all of eternity.

After understanding what the gospel is, now we understand better why it is described in our key text as the "gospel of peace". The gospel gives us the peace **of** God and peace **with** God. **Philippians 4:7** says, *"And the peace of God, which passeth all understanding, shall keep your hearts and minds through Christ Jesus."* The peace of God gives us an unfeigned assurance in God that keeps us from being anxious and double-minded in challenging situations. Yet, we have access to the peace of God, because we have peace with God. **Romans 5:1** says, *"Therefore being justified by faith, we have peace with God through our Lord Jesus Christ:"* Before being saved, we were enemies against God which put us in danger of the wrath of God. But now we have peace with God through accepting the blessed gospel of Jesus Christ. There are two types of peace we have as children of God. We have the peace **of** God and peace **with** God. After having peace **with** God we can then experience the peace **of** God.

The Gospel of Peace counteracts the kingdom of Satan, which wants people to live against the will of God and in the spirit of fear. Satan holds people hostage to the cares of this life, the social systems that govern the world and sin which is now at an all time high. The gospel message will give individuals the peace that passes understanding because they will enter into an assured victory through the blood of Jesus. People who are being held captive by the devil need peace. People don't need condemnation or judgment, but the peace that acceptance of the gospel will give. Thus, Satan keeps men and women in darkness from the gospel. The gospel is light and any man who believes the gospel cannot remain in darkness. Only unbelief of the gospel can keep men and women in darkness; thereby rendering them powerless to Satan and his devices. In his confrontation of the heretical teachings of Erasmus, Martin Luther makes a powerful case of the simplicity and plain clarity of the gospel. He states, *"If our gospel be hid, it is hid to them that are lost, whose heart the god of this world hath blinded"* (2 Cor. 4. 3-4). *They are like men who cover their eyes, or go from daylight into darkness, and hid there, and then blame the sun, or the darkness of the day, for their inability to see. So let wretched men abjure that blasphemous perversity which would blame the darkness of their own hearts on the plain Scriptures of God!"* [12] *pg. 72.* As a believer, if you decide to exist in any other ritualism, culture, or tradition that is not entrenched in the truth of the gospel, you have no excuse for your life of darkness.

The gospel is a weapon that must be used effectively and continuously. Paul states in **Romans 1:16**, *"For I am not ashamed of the gospel of Christ; for it is the power of God unto salvation to everyone that believeth; to the Jew first, and also to the Greek."* I am saved through the gospel which explains the importance of having my feet wrapped and prepared with it. Please note that the gospel is the "power of God". It is the conduit or channel by which His creation accesses salvation.

Therefore, the preparation of the gospel of peace is a powerful weapon against the enemy's kingdom. All of our intellect, sciences, philosophies, and personal ideals do nothing against the kingdom of Satan. It is only the essence of the gospel that can pull down strongholds and destroy the kingdom of Satan.

---

[12] Luther, Martin. "The Bondage Of The Will"-Translated by Packer and Johnston. Revell (1957). Grand Rapids, MI

Anytime Satan tries to create doubt, fear, confusion, or anxiety, the believer must focus their attention on the cross. Anytime Satan tries to discourage, create depression or unbelief, we must focus our attention on the glorious gospel of Jesus Christ. Thus, we must remain prepared in the knowledge of the depth of the gospel and be ready to use that knowledge and conviction to stand against the kingdom of Satan.

SHIELD OF FAITH

"Above all, taking the shield of faith, wherewith ye shall be able to quench all the fiery darts of the wicked."

Paul is simply telling us to use our faith at all times. Many scholars have studied Paul's statement concerning the shield of faith and the type of visual picture he wanted the Ephesians to obtain. During this time, soldiers would carry shields that were very large. The shield would be large enough for a soldier to kneel behind and be totally protected from arrows. The shield also had a sharp tip at the bottom so that the soldier could dig it down into the dirt for extra security. Often times, when armies went out to war, they would line up the soldiers with the shields fortified in the ground. This would create a blockade that the enemy could not destroy easily and a barrier that the archers could hide behind, waiting for the right time to shoot back at the enemy. Your faith alone is big enough to quench all the fiery darts of the enemy. No matter what goes on in your life, you must totally depend and trust in the word of God.

Faith is the Kingdom's currency. It is the mode by which all transactions take place in the Kingdom. You cannot obtain anything in the Kingdom without faith. Your armor will be useless without faith. You cannot be saved without faith. You can't receive any of the covenant benefits without faith. You can't do any great work for God without faith. There is absolutely nothing that you can do in the Kingdom without faith, because faith is the spiritual currency by which everything in the Kingdom occurs. You will be able to stop the devil right in his tracks with your faith. There will be a blockade protecting your vision, family, and career goals when you operate in the spiritual power of faith.

Hebrews 11:1 says, *"Faith is the substance of things hoped for, the evidence of things not seen."* If faith is "the substance", then without it you have nothing solid to use to engage in spiritual transactions. Faith is the evidence. In science, no theory is accepted without evidence. The same is true in the Kingdom of God. Faith is "the evidence" of things hoped for. Without faith, you have no evidence that what you are praying for, have received in God, or will do in God is legitimate. Therefore, faith is the substance and the evidence believers use to stand sure in the things of God.

[181]

Now I must caution you, there is a movement of error in the Body of Christ. This movement is encouraging people to have "Faith in Faith" or "Faith in Self Thought". Believers are engaging in a false idea that faith means we speak whatever we want, believe that it will happen and it will. These believers who have been taught this false teaching are claiming possession of things that they have no spiritual right to. This type of teaching amounts to nothing more than humanist teachings that denies the power of God. This error leads to disappointments and further error when the things that they believe for don't happen. God never told us to have faith in faith, but to have faith in Him, which is represented by His will, purpose and word. Just because you claim something to be yours, does not make it so. The words that we speak as children of God are from our God. Our God is spirit and therefore His word in its initial state is spirit. Jesus said, *"The Spirit gives life; the flesh counts for nothing. The words I have spoken to you are spirit and they are life"* **(John 6:63)**. Therefore, when I receive a word from God it is spiritual and it produces real spirit born faith.

Romans 10:17 says, *"Faith cometh by hearing, and hearing by the word of God."* God's word is spirit, which produces spiritual hearing and revelation, which in turn produces spiritual faith. It is the sending of God's word that produces hearing. If His word is not sent, then man will remain in darkness concerning his God and purpose. When man hears the word of God, faith is produced. This faith can then be used to make spiritual transactions. When the believer walks in the spirit, they will be able to *"decree a thing, and it shall be established; and the light shall be upon thy ways"* **Job 22:28.** Declarations of God's word are spirit and life. Therefore, we speak the word of God in faith and watch the establishing of what God has ordained. When I have an open ear to hear what God is uttering and speaking, I can then speak. God speaks, we hear, and then we speak. Some individuals who have misinterpreted the "faith movement" have been led to believe that whatever they speak, God must honor. This is not true. God only honors His word and will. Although we might think we can operate under our own strength, God has the last say on all things that are true and pure. Thus, God honors His word, which is why He gives it to us so that we can engage in effective spiritual warfare.

Paul continues in **Hebrews 11:6,** *"But without faith it is impossible to please him..."* God cannot be pleased with us as believers if we are not walking in faith. God cannot be approached without faith. God cannot be approached by intellect, emotion, or "hear say". God is offended when His own children doubt His promises and word. God cannot get any glory or pleasure out of any actions taken by His children that are not born out of faith. **Habakkuk 2:4** *says, "Behold, his soul which is lifted up is not upright in him: but the just shall live by his faith."* Note that the soul of this man is not upright within his own ability. Therefore, he must live by his faith. Faith is the source of life for the believer. There can be no life in God without faith. We cannot trust in our ability to do anything for God or in God. **Romans 1:17** sums up the context by which the believer must live by when Paul says, *"For therein (the gospel) is the righteousness of God reveled from faith to faith: as it is written, the just shall live by faith."* Thus, no matter what situation we come from or are currently in, if we find our refuge in the gospel and the word of God, He will move us from dimension to dimension in Him. When we begin to move into the various dimensions of faith that God has for us, we will be able to be proactive in spiritual warfare. We will have the ability to believe God for the great things that He has shown are ours through His word. Paul emphasizes living by faith again in **Hebrews 10:38**, but also focuses on the danger of not living by faith. He states, *"Now the just shall live by faith: but if any man draw back, my soul shall have no pleasure in him."* Believers who have faith one minute and then start doubting the next minute are not ready for warfare. As believers, we must have consistent, stable faith that does not draw back or doubt. The enemy sends circumstances and obstacles to try to get the believer to draw back on their faith because he knows that a believer who walks in faith will be able to do great exploits in the spirit.

There are many examples of faith in the scriptures. Here are a few that may help you begin to move in a greater level of faith. After each scriptural example, there is a summative statement presented to give understanding of the lesson that should be taken from the scriptural text.

Matthew 8:6-8   *"And saying, Lord, my servant lieth at home sick of the palsy, grievously tormented. And Jesus saith unto him, I will come and heal him. The centurion answered and said, Lord, I am not worthy that thou shouldest come under my roof: but speak the word only, and my servant shall be healed."*

~Our faith can send the word into any situation and get the results God intended for us to obtain.

Matthew 17:20   *"And Jesus said unto them, Because of your unbelief: for verily I say unto you, If ye have faith as a grain of mustard seed, ye shall say unto this mountain, Remove hence to yonder place; and it shall remove; and nothing shall be impossible unto you."*

~Pure faith of small quantity is enough to do the impossible. It is not about the size of the faith, as much as it is about the purity of the faith.

Mark 5:25-34   *"And a certain woman, which had an issue of blood twelve years, and had suffered many things of many physicians, and had spent all that she had, and was nothing bettered, but rather grew worse. When she had heard of Jesus, came in the press behind, and touched his garment. For she said, If I may touch but his clothes (hem or border of garment), I shall be whole.*

[185]

And straightway the fountain of her blood was dried up; and she felt in her body that she was healed of that plaque. And Jesus, immediately knowing in himself that virtue had gone out of him, turned him about in the press, and said, Who touched my clothes: And his disciples said unto him, thou seest the multitude thronging thee, and sayest thou, Who touched me? And he looked round about to see her that had done this thing. But the woman fearing and trembling, knowing what was done in her, came and fell down before him, and told him all the truth. And he said unto her. Daughter, thy faith hath made thee whole; go in peace, and be whole of thy plague."

~Faith will push you to move outside your limits and situations to get what you need from God. Faith creates faith. It causes us to see God's will in all situations and pursue His will with great conviction and persuasion.

Matthew 15:22-28   *"And, behold, a woman of Canaan came out of the same coasts, and cried unto him, saying, Have mercy on me, O Lord, thou son of David: my daughter is grievously vexed with a devil. But he answered her not a word. And his disciples came and besought him, saying, Send her away: for she crieth after us. But he answered and said, I am not sent but unto the lost sheep of the house of Israel. Then came she and worshipped him, saying, Lord, help me. But he answered and said, It is not meet to take the children's bread, and to cast it to dogs. And she said, Truth, Lord; yet the dogs* *eat of the crumbs which fall from their master' table. Then Jesus answered and said unto her, O woman, great is thy faith; be it unto thee even as thou wilt. And her daughter was made whole from that very hour."*

~Faith bypasses the rules that govern the natural world or social systems. Faith will seek Jesus until the answer, miracle, or blessing is released. Faith has no concern about the opinions of natural men. Faith is focused and determined.

Mark 16:17-18   *"And these signs shall follow them that believe; In my name shall they cast out devils; they shall speak with new tongues; They shall take up serpents; and if they drink any deadly thing, it shall not hurt them; they shall lay hands on the sick, and they shall recover."*

~Faith gives you access to power with God. This power will be manifested through gifts and signs which can be used to destroy the devil's kingdom, insulate the child of God from the attacks of the devil, and minister to people in need.

James 5:15   *"And the prayer of faith shall save the sick, and the Lord shall raise him up; and if he have committed sins, they shall be forgiven him."*

~Faith can heal any sickness and stop any negative situation or circumstance no matter how long it's been in

[187]

existence. Faith gives the believer access to forgiveness.

Remember, the just shall live by faith (Romans 1:17). The key word is live. Everything that we do must be done through faith. We enter the Body through faith, we receive the gifts of God through faith, and we are sustained and developed through faith. Anything that is not done in faith is sin for the believer. **Romans 14:23 states, "...*For whatsoever is not of faith is sin.*"** Many times ministers give up on their ministry because of situations and circumstances that have arisen. People get divorces, quit jobs, and leave churches because they have lost faith in the initial promise of God. Reader, you must believe God above all contrary circumstances because circumstances are only temporary, but the word of God shall remain forever. When we begin to walk in faith, we understand and have confidence that when the word of God is spoken, things will happen. We walk in a power that most only wish about. We have complete victory.

THE WHOLE ARMOR OF GOD

Part 2

THE HELMET OF SALVATION

"And take the helmet of salvation and the sword of the spirit, which is the word of God." **(Ephesians 6:17)**

We must constantly protect our thoughts and motives with the helmet or covering of salvation. The mind controls all of the activities of the body. You are your mind. **Proverb 23:7** says, *"For as he thinketh in his heart, so is he..."* You become the expression of your thoughts and therefore must protect your mind at all cost. A believer that allows things into their mind without discretion is playing with fire. Our minds must be renewed daily and protected with salvation and deliverance. For the purposes of warfare, I will deal with salvation from the perspective of being a disciple of Christ. You have to know without a shadow of a doubt that you are saved. In an attempt to overthrow your authority in God, the devil will attack you in your mind concerning your salvation. The logic is simple, if you are not saved, or are not sure that you are saved, you will never have the audacity to stand up and fight against the devil. When I know and declare that I am saved, I am saying that I have entered into the new covenant benefits of the Kingdom of God which includes having authority over every demonic entity, the flesh, and wicked system in existence.

The believer puts on the helmet of salvation to guard their mind from the lies and deceitful persuasions of the enemy. If the devil can take control of your thought patterns, there will be a breech in communication between you and God. This is why children of God should ask God every day to renew their mind and cleanse their thoughts. **Romans 12:2** *says, "And be not conformed to this world: but be ye transformed by the renewing of your mind, that you may prove what is that good, and acceptable, and perfect will of God."* I cannot prove or show the will of God in my life if my mind is not renewed. If your mind is full of toxic waste you will express those things that are not in the will of God and therefore cease to be effective in giving Him glory. Your mind is the root of every action you make and is the ultimate battle ground of spiritual warfare. The Holy Spirit helps individuals fight the temptations of Satan through empowerment in their thought process. Your mind is such a vital resource in spiritual warfare, that the Lord will allow you to go through horrific situations just to cause you to turn your mind to Him. It is through the mind by which God will install the tenacity, creativity, insight, wisdom, and strength for you to walk in His power and favor.

If you are constantly watching television, listening to secular things, and associating with the world, it may become extremely difficult to control many of your actions. When an individual wants to fight spiritually, there must be spiritual content present to fight with. In other words, if you have not equipped your mind for war through the reading of God's word, prayer, and meditation, when the enemy comes to oppose you, your life may be overwhelmed. Therefore, wear the helmet of Salvation or the helmet of God's principles, promises, and laws concerning our salvation, so that you can defeat the devil as soon as he confronts you.

THE WORD OF GOD

Next, Paul said that we should take the sword of the Spirit. This sword of the spirit is the word of God. If this word comes out of the spirit, it must also be spirit in its content. Jesus is the living word. **John 1:1** says, *"In the beginning was the Word, and the Word was with God, and the Word was God."* In describing Jesus, John uses the Greek word *"logos"* which means *words uttered by a living voice which embodies the concept or idea.* It is God and God's thought. It is God and God's motive. It is God and God's expressed idea. Wow, our Lord and Savior Jesus Christ is awesome!

[191]

What a mighty God we serve. The word Paul uses in Ephesians 6:17 is different though. The Greek word used is *"rhema"* which means *that which is or has been uttered by the living voice, thing spoken, or any sound produced by the voice with definite meaning.* Thus, this verse is not just encouraging us to read through the Bible. Rather, it deals with us allowing God to breathe life into the scriptures. When we carry the divine utterances of God, we have power with God in "real time".

Current technology has advanced to the place where there doesn't have to be a delay in sent communication. With just the touch of a button, an email, text, or video can be sent with a delay time so small that it is unnoticeable to the average human. Technology is only beginning to catch up with where God has always been. When God speaks, it is delivered right now in real time. If we are walking in the spirit, we will be downloaded with divine utterances and direction from God continually. It is the divine utterance of God that gives us power over the enemy. When you declare what God has promised you, you are expressing your faith, which has the power to create and bring to fruition what God has ordained.

All that we do as children of God should be based on the word of God. There is no need for opinion or speculation. The question should always be, "What does God say about it?" The word of God is the beginning and the end of all matters. In *The Purpose Driven Life*, by Pastor Rick Warren, the truth concerning spiritual growth is identified as being solely in the child of God's ability to eat and digest the word of God. Pastor Rick Warren states, *"The spirit of God uses the Word of God to make us like the Son of God...The Bible is far more than a doctrinal guidebook. God's Word generates life, creates faith, produces change, frightens the Devil, causes miracles, heals hurts, builds character, transforms circumstances, imparts joy, overcomes adversity, defeats temptation, infuses hope, releases power, cleanses our minds, brings things into being, and guarantees our future forever!"* [13]*pg. 185-186.* Wow, what glorious illumination. We have victory through God's word.

We should not seek to memorize a lot of verses without meditation and prayer. Memorization of scripture is good, but if the Spirit doesn't breathe life into them and give you revelation, you will not know how to properly use them for living purposes and spiritual warfare. We should seek to apply scriptures to our lives according to the leading of the Holy Spirit, which will give us victory and abundant life. The devil will war against your identity in God or attempt to make you doubt God's plan for your life. The devil will try to make you believe that God won't heal you, save your children or protect you. This is why the word is so important. The word gives us assurance that we will be blessed and that the war we are waging is already won. The word of God should be utilized in all areas of spiritual

---

[13] Warren, Rick. "The Purpose Driven Life". Zondervan (2002). Grand Rapids, Michigan

warfare. Here are some questions the devil may attempt to place in your mind and a few scriptures to help you cast down those discouragements. Reader, fight the devil with the word of God!

1. **How do I know if I have entered into the Body of Christ? Is confession enough? Is baptism all it takes? Am I saved?**

This is a question that I have been asked by so many over the years. The devil will try to make the believer feel unsure of their salvation and begin to live in guilt, fear, and doubt. Guilt, fear and doubt will paralyze a believer and make them unproductive in the kingdom. Remember believer, no matter what your denominational background or persuasion, salvation has been secured by the works of Christ and is received through faith. Everything hangs on our faith. Here are some scriptures that will give you the assurance you need, not only for your salvation, but to use in spiritual warfare against the enemy when he tries to make you doubt your salvation. These scriptures can also be used as a witnessing tool.

Matthew 28:19   *"Go ye therefore, and teach all nations, baptizing them in the name of the Father, and of the Son, and of the Holy Ghost."*

Jesus commands the apostles to go into the world and teach all nations (people) His teachings which emphasize the culture, language, principles and

[194]

laws of the Kingdom of God. The sanctioned act that memorializes the regeneration experience is baptism, which is commanded to be done in the name of the Father, and Son and Holy Spirit; Jesus. *(The name of Jesus will be discussed in greater depth in chapter 11).*

Mark 16:16   *"He that believeth and is baptized shall be saved; be he that believeth not shall be damned."*

Jesus emphatically states in this passage that he that believes (with the faith that comes from hearing the word of God) and is baptized (which is the sanctioned ceremonial act expressing to the public the conversion experience that has taken place in the heart) a person will be saved. Please note that if one doesn't believe, they are already condemned. Belief is the key.

Luke 24:47   *"And that repentance and remission of sins should be preached in his name among all nations, beginning at Jerusalem."*

The call to repentance from sin and belief in Jesus was commanded to be preached in His (Jesus') name. Jesus' name is used because it signifies that it is not being done by the authority of the speaker, but by His authority and under His kingship since He is the purchaser and propitiation for the salvation of all humanity. The fulfillment of this verse of scripture happened on the day of Pentecost in Acts chapter 2. At that time, repentance and remission of sins was preached.

John 3:5   *"Jesus answered, Verily, verily, I say unto thee, Except a man be born of water and of the Spirit, he cannot enter into the Kingdom of God."*

Contrary to popular belief, the water spoken of here is not about the birth water that a baby is in when born, but rather the waters of baptism in Jesus' name and infilling of the Holy Spirit which is God's earnest inheritance of His glory. The Holy Spirit is God's endorsement of the conversion experience which takes place in the heart and faith toward Him.

Acts 1:8   *"But ye shall receive power <u>after</u> that the Holy Ghost is come upon you: and ye shall be witnesses unto me both in Jerusalem and in all Judea, and in Samaria, and unto the uttermost part of the earth."*

All those who believe in God and have faith in His blessed Son, shall receive power to be witnesses. The child of God is "made" a witness by the Holy Spirit and also given the ability to minister to a dying world.

Acts 2:1-4   *"And when the day of Pentecost was fully come, they were all with one accord in one place. And* *suddenly there came a sound from heaven as of a rushing mighty wind, and it filled all the house where they were sitting. And there appeared unto them cloven tongues like as of fire, and it sat upon each of them. And they were all filled with the Holy Ghost, and began to speak with other tongues, as the Spirit gave them utterance."*

Acts 2:37-38   *"Now when they heard this, they were pricked in their heart, and said unto Peter and to the rest of the apostles, Men and brethren, what shall we do? Then Peter said unto them, Repent, and be baptized every one of you in the name of Jesus Christ for the remission of sins, and ye shall receive the gift of the Holy Ghost."*

Acts 4:12   *"Neither is there salvation in any other: for there is none other* name *under heaven given among men, whereby we must be saved."*

Acts 8:12-17   *"But when they believed Phillip preaching the things concerning the Kingdom of God, and the name of Jesus Christ, they were baptized, both men and women. Then Simon himself* believed also: *and when he was baptized, he continued with Phillip, and wondered, beholding the miracles and signs which were done. Now when the apostles which were at Jerusalem heard that Samaria had received the word of God, they sent unto them Peter and John: Who, when they were come down, prayed for them, that they might receive the Holy Ghost: (For as yet he was fallen upon none of them:* only they were *baptized in the name of the Lord Jesus.) Then laid they their hands on them, and they* received *the Holy Ghost."*

Acts 9:17-18   *"And Ananias went his way, and entered into the house; and putting his hands on him said, Brother Saul, the Lord, even Jesus, that appeared unto thee in the way as thou camest, hath sent me, that thou mightest receive thy sight, and be filled with the Holy Ghost. And immediately there fell from his eyes as it had been scales: and he received sight forthwith, and arose, and was baptized."*

Romans 8:9   *"But ye are not in the flesh, but in the Spirit, if so be that the Spirit of God dwell in you. Now if any man have not the Spirit of Christ, he is none of his."*

Romans 10:9   *"That if thou shalt confess with thy mouth the Lord Jesus and shalt believe in thine heart that God hath raised him from the dead, thou shalt be saved."*

Ephesians 4:5-6   *"One Lord, one faith, one baptism, One God and Father of all who is above all, and through all, and in you all."*

Believer, you have assurance through the word of God that you are saved and redeemed by our Lord and Savior Jesus Christ. The enemy will try to cause you to act in a manner that is unfit for a child of God by making you doubt your salvation. You are sealed, stamped and ready to be delivered (raptured). For further study, also read Acts 10:44-48, 16:15, 32,33, 18:8, 19:1-6; Romans 6:3-4, 10: 13; 1 Corinthians 10:1-2,

[198]

12:13; Galatians 3:10-14, 26-28; Ephesians 2: 4-10; Colossians 2:11-12; Hebrews 6:1-3; 1 Peter 3:20-21.

2. Is it God's will for me to be healed?

Sickness is a part of human existence. Our bodies will not last forever and depending on our ancestral background and life choices, our bodies deteriorate at slow or fast paces. It is God's will for his children to live in health. Yet, the believer should understand that they will receive a new body anyway, when they cross over into eternity. With that said, it is important that believers seek the healing of God when sickness comes in their life. Some sicknesses are caused by sin, some are by unhealthy life choices, and some are direct acts by the devil. The following scriptures should be used to combat sickness.

Exodus 15:26   *"And said, If thou wilt diligently hearken to the voice of the Lord thy God, and wilt do that which is right in his sight, and wilt give ear to his commandments, and keep all his statutes, I will put none of these diseases upon thee, which I have brought upon the Egyptians: for I am the Lord that healeth thee."*

Psalms 118:17   *"I shall not die, but live, and declare the works of the Lord."*

Isaiah 53:5   *"But he was wounded for our transgressions, he was bruised for our iniquities: the chastisement of our peace was upon him; and with his* *stripes we are healed."*

Matthew 8:2-3   *"And, behold, there came a leper and worshipped him, saying, Lord, if thou wilt, thou canst make me clean. And Jesus put forth his hand, and touched him, saying, I will: be thou clean. And immediately his leprosy was cleansed."*

Matthew 9:20-22   *"And, behold, a woman, which was diseased with an issue of blood twelve years came behind him, and touched the hem of his garment: For she said within herself, If I may but touch his garment, I shall be whole. But Jesus turned him about, and when he saw her he said, Daughter, be of good comfort; thy faith hath made thee whole. And the woman was made whole from that hour."*

Luke 9:11   *"And the people when they knew it, followed him: and he received them, and spake unto them of the Kingdom of God, and healed them that had need of healing."*

James 5:13-15   *"Is any among you afflicted? Let him pray. Is any merry? Let him sing psalms. Is any sick among you? Let him call for the elders of the church; and let them pray over him, anointing him with oil in the name of the Lord: And the prayer of faith shall save the sick, and the Lord shall raise him up; and if he have committed sins, they shall be forgiven him."*

3. I'm dealing with a lot of confusion and frustration. Can the Lord give me direction?

There is a large array of problems that the devil will send into your life in order to distract you from reaching your destiny in God. When the devil does this, it is usually because he can sense God working in your life, or he wants to keep you from your mission in God. Confusion unravels slowly into a web of choices and decisions that need to be made. The devil wants the problem to seem out of your ability to control. When we are overwhelmed, we will often reach out for anything to help get some relief. The enemy will then move in for the kill, causing you to make even worse decisions. God wants the believer to seek Him for direction so that they can walk in wisdom. By walking in the wisdom of God, we are saved from decisions and circumstances that can be detrimental physically, emotionally, economically and definitely spiritually. These scriptures should be used to help you stay on track, so that you can continue to wage war against the enemy.

Proverbs 4:7   *"Wisdom is the principal thing; therefore get wisdom; and with all thy getting get understanding."*

John 16:13   *"Howbeit when he, the Spirit of truth, is come, he will guide you into all truth: for he shall not speak of himself; but whatsoever he shall hear, that shall he speak: and he will shew you things to come."*

1 Corinthians 2:10   *"But God hath revealed them unto us by his Spirit: for the Spirit searcheth all things, yea, the deep things of God."*

1 Corinthians 14:33 *"For God is not the author of confusion, but of peace, as in all churches of the saints."*

Phillipians 4:6-7   *"Be careful for nothing; but in everthing by prayer and supplication with thanksgiving let your request be made known unto God. And the peace of God, which passeth all understanding, shall keep your hearts and minds through Christ Jesus."*

James 1:5   *"If any of you lack wisdom, let him ask of God, that giveth to all men liberally, and upbraideth not; and it shall be given him."*

4. **What does God say about my enemies and people who are against me?**

Quite frankly, I don't give a lot of concern to people who are supposedly against me. I don't think that the believer should dwell on the people or entities that may not be supporting or are even against them. I hear a lot of preachers get people to focus on people as if that is some great victory. You should be focused on God's mission for you and allow Him to deal with your supposed enemies. As stated earlier, we only have one real enemy and that is the devil. Therefore, I must see all controversial and conflicting situations with people as manifestations of the enemy and opportunities for God to get the glory. Here are a few scriptures that will encourage you should you face opposition from people.

Genesis 12:3   *"And I will bless them that bless thee, and curse him that curseth thee: and in thee shall all families of the earth be blessed."*

Deuteronomy 28:7 *"The Lord shall cause thine enemies that rise up against thee to be smitten before thy face: they shall come out against thee one way, and flee before thee seven ways."*

Psalms 27:2   *"When the wicked, even mine enemies and my foes, came upon me to eat up my flesh, they stumbled and fell."*

Isaiah 54:17   *"No weapon that is formed against thee shall prosper; and every tongue that shall rise against thee in judgment thou shalt condemn. This is the heritage of the servants of the Lord, and their righteousness is of me, saith the Lord."*

Matthew 5:44   *"But I say unto you, Love your enemies, bless them that curse you, do good to them that hate you, and pray for them which despitefully use you, and persecute you;"*

Romans 12:19-20   *"Dearly beloved, avenge not yourselves, but rather give place unto wrath: for it is written, Vengeance* *is mine: I will repay, saith the Lord.   Therefore if thine enemy hunger, feed him; if he thirst, give him drink: for in so doing thou shalt heap coals of fire on his head."*

5. I only have a little bit of money and a lot of month left! What do I do?

There is so much stress placed on money in our modern day world, that some believers have become numb to the fact that our God is the God of everything. I heard one report that suggested that most divorces take place because of problems with money. Many in the Kingdom live outside their means and pursue worldly possessions which can often times cause them to struggle to meet their very basic needs. However, there are situations that arise that are out of our control or that the Lord is delivering us from. We must know as believers that our God is our supplier and will provide us with the things we need in life. As the believer becomes faithful in their financial stewardship to the Kingdom of God, lives in moderation, and is a cheerful giver, God will open up doors of provision for them. Here are a few scriptures that you can use to stand against the devil when he tries to create financial stress or the spirit of poverty over your life.

Deuteronomy 28:2-5*"And all these blessings shall come on thee, and overtake thee, if thou shalt hearken unto the voice of the LORD thy God. Blessed [shalt] thou be in the city, and blessed shalt thou [be] in the field. Blessed [shall be] the* fruit of thy body, and the fruit of thy ground, and the fruit of thy cattle, the increase of thy kine, and the flocks of thy sheep. Blessed shalt thou be when thou comest in, and blessed shalt thou [be] when thou goest out."

Joshua 1:3   "Every place that the sole of your foot shall tread upon, that have I given unto you, as said unto Moses."

Psalms 24:1   "The earth is the LORD'S, and the fullness thereof; the world, and they that dwell therein."

Psalms 37:25   "I have been young, and now am old; yet have I not seen the righteous forsaken, nor his seed begging bread."

Hosea 2: 8   "The silver is mine, and the gold is mine, saith the LORD of hosts."

Matthew 6: 30-33   "Wherefore, if God so clothe the grass of the field, which today is, and tomorrow is cast into the oven, [shall he] not much more [clothe] you, O ye of little faith? Therefore take no thought, saying, What shall we eat? or, What shall we drink? or, Wherewithal shall we be clothed? (For after all these things do the Gentiles seek:) for your heavenly Father knoweth that ye have need of all these things. But seek ye first the Kingdom of God, and his righteousness; and all these things shall be added unto you."

Philipians 4:19   "But my God shall supply all your need *according to his riches in glory by Christ Jesus."*

3 John 2   *"Beloved, I wish above all things that thou mayest prosper and be in health, even as thy soul prospereth."*

SUMMARY OF THE WORD

This is only a small portion of scriptures that can help you stand up against the attacks of Satan. In order to build up your faith, you must consistently study the word of God and continually speak the word, meditate on the word, and pray the word so that it will become a part of your being. Once again, the Bible says, *"For as he thinketh in his heart, so is he..."* **(Proverbs 23:7).** Therefore, if you embrace the word of God, making it a part of your fibers and being, you will become a walking, living power. When you saturate yourself in the word of God, you are able to engage in spiritual warfare spontaneously. Many believers wait to make it back to church, or call their minister, or wait on an altar call to engage in spiritual warfare. Yet, because of the high intensity and continuous warring taking place in the spirit realm, the believer needs to be ready to fight at all times.

The believer's root and stability is in the word of God. **Psalms 1:2** states, *"But his delight is in the law of the Lord; and in his law doth he meditate day and night. And he shall be like a tree planted by the rivers of water..."* We must delight ourselves in the word so that we can become strong in the things of God. The writer says we will be like a tree. Think about that. In spiritual warfare, we cannot be unstable, wavering, or unsure. We must be like a tree whose roots run so deep that no matter what storm comes our way, we will be able to withstand it. Some of the oldest and strongest trees in the world are in California; the Sequoia Redwoods. At first glance, it would seem that the key ingredient to these trees long existence and unshakable strength is their size or root depth. But, it is not strength or size that has allowed these trees to exist for thousands of years. These trees have strong roots that intertwine with one another. Each tree is founded in the trees around it which make them an unmovable wonder on God's earth. We, too, are unmovable when we are founded in the word. Our roots intertwine with truth, wisdom, revelation, and power, setting the stage for victory over the enemy.

Discussions, Reflections, and Activities

1. Paul admonishes us to "put on the whole armor". Identify each piece of armor and explain the purpose of the armor and weapon.

2. Discuss three ideas that stood out to you in this chapter. Why is it important? How do you relate to it?

3. Discuss a time when you lost your faith in something or someone. What caused you to lose your faith?

4. If you only had one piece of armor to choose from,

which piece would you choose? Why?

5. Paul admonishes us to put on the breastplate of righteousness. Discuss the difference between self-righteousness and God's righteousness.

6. Research: Choose three scriptures for each piece of the whole armor. The purpose of these scriptures will be to commit to memory, so that you can be prepared for warfare.

Notes:

_____

_____

_____

_____

_____

_____

_____

_____

_____

_____

_____

_____

_____

"Pray without ceasing."

I Thessalonians 5:17

Chapter 10

PRAYER, FASTING & MEDITATION

In **Ephesians 6:18** Paul finishes his discussion of the Whole Armor by admonishing us to pray. Verse 18 says,

"Praying- always with all prayer and supplication in the Spirit, and watching whereunto with all perseverance and supplication for all saints"

Prayer is the language of the Kingdom of God. It is the keyboard that faith types on in order to give the believer access into the power of God, the covenant blessings, and mysteries in the heavenlies. Prayer is the vehicle that carries

[209]

faith and faith is the fuel of the vehicle. All fuel must be carried in the vehicle that it fuels. The same is true for prayer and faith. Prayer is the action that God has both sanctioned and endorsed as the essential weapon of the believer along with the word of God. Prayer is the means by which we make our request known in the Kingdom of God. Just as one would go to the city court house, fill out forms for a government agency, or send a letter to an elected official, the believer uses prayer as their means of communicating to the King of the Kingdom. The only difference between the above example and how we as believers operate is the fact that as children of God, we are not in a democracy, but citizens of a kingdom. We can never take to the streets and boycott, because we are in a kingdom that is run by a sovereign King, who has established Kingdom rules, and a process by which all things in the Kingdom exist. Our King makes sure that all of our needs are met.

Prayer is the act of petitioning or making a request. Yet, it is important that the believer understand that prayer can be used for more than just making requests to God for the average, mundane happenings of life. Prayer can be used to engage in spiritual warfare and do damage to the enemy's kingdom. The Bible teaches us that prayer through faith is a vital part of spiritual warfare. Paul admonished and encouraged us in **I Thessalonians 5:17** to *"Pray without ceasing."* Because spiritual warfare is an ongoing reality, children of God must never cease to pray. It is impossible for us to be on our knees twenty-four hours a day, but we can remain in a posture of prayer always. Being in the posture of prayer means that I am always conscious of what is happening in the natural and spiritual realm and ready to pray. I keep myself clean and available to engage in prayer. While doing my work on a daily basis, I can engage in spiritual warfare on behalf of my office environment, disputes between co-workers, and the overall productivity of the company the Lord has blessed me to work for. When I am in a posture of prayer, I don't drive pass an accident on the freeway and just look for shock value. I pass by and begin praying for the individuals in the accident, their families and their salvation. Thus, "praying without ceasing" becomes a lifestyle and a culture that children of God live by and operate in.

God has given us a distinct and everlasting promise concerning prayer. God leaves no room for us to doubt the power and effects of prayer. The enemy also knows these promises and has therefore done all he can to stop the children of God from praying. Church services are packed with singing, commentary, announcements, and recognitions of dignitaries, but very little prayer. Children of God claim to want to see the power of God move in a mighty way, but it will require great sacrifice in prayer in order for that to happen. In many churches, there is not even a time set aside for prayer. Prayer is also one of the lowest attended services in churches. Many church programs are full of activities that don't involve prayer. Many churches have even given up on trying to get young people to pray, giving in to a lot of light weight programs that massage the social development of young people, but not their spiritual development. These realities are detrimental to the Body of Christ. We must fight for prayer and make it an absolute priority in our personal lives and corporate assemblies. The Lord says in **2 Chronicles 7:14** *"If my people who are called by my name would humble themselves and pray, and seek my face and turn from their wicked ways. Then will I hear from heaven, I will forgive their sins and heal their land."*

Once again we see the importance of this book's title and theme, "Our Warfare". God says, *"If my people"*. There are no lone soldiers in the promise. God is expecting a unified revival in prayer. Also note the cause and effect relationship the Lord presents. The Lord provides an *"If"* statement and a *"Then"* statement. This is the science of prayer. It is the formula by which a heavenly transaction is made. The Lord gives us four things to do: humble, pray, seek, and turn. Humble, pray, seek, and turn is the causal statement. The effect is threefold: He'll hear, forgive, and heal. Wow, what a powerful promise. The Lord is waiting for the people of God to come to Him in prayer, so that the blessings stored for them can be released. Believer, the healing of a nation rests in the prayer lives of the children of God. The favor of a nation rests in the prayer lives of the children of God. The longevity of a nation rests in the prayer lives of the children of God. The economic wealth of a nation rests in the prayer lives of the children of God. The protection of a nation rests in the prayer lives of the children of God. Everything that our world, nation and families need is wrapped up in the prayer lives of the children of God.

THE DISCIPLE'S PRAYER

The most popular illustration of prayer in scripture is what is commonly known as "The Lord's Prayer". In actuality, this is the disciple's prayer, because it was the disciples who asked the Lord to teach them how to pray. The disciple's prayer is a guide. It is not given to be used as an end all to prayer. In **Matthew 6:9-13**, Jesus points out six keys that make prayer effective. The six keys are worship, seeking God's will, seeking provision for needs, forgiveness, deliverance from the evil of the enemy, and doxology or worship to God. The first thing we should do when we enter into prayer is acknowledge God as our holy Father. Before asking God for anything, we should give God glory and honor for what He has done and for who He is. Statements acknowledging Him as Creator, Eternal and the Only Living God are statements of worship. Statements acknowledging Him as Provider, Savior, Redeemer and good to us are statements of praise. Second, we should then seek for God's will to be done. This shows God that we accept His sovereignty and right to do what He wants to do in all matters. Jesus says, *"Thy kingdom come. Thy will be done in earth, as it is in heaven"* in **verse 10**. We should seek for God's kingdom to be made manifested in our daily lives. Through prayer, we don't have to accept the realities of this life, but can move in the reality of the Kingdom which supersedes the happenings of the systems of this world. Third, we should ask God to provide us with our daily needs. God promises to provide us with our daily needs. Please note that this may not include some of our wants, but

[213]

God will take care of His children. King David says, *"...yet have I not seen the righteous forsaken, nor his seed begging bread"* **(Psalms 37:25)**. It is God's desire to give provision for His children and that they would prosper in Him.

The Lord then hones in on a major point He wanted to emphasize to His disciples, which is the need for forgiveness and to forgive. He says, *"And forgive us our debts, as we forgive our debtors"* **(Matthew 6:12)**. One of the major purposes of prayer is to ask God for forgiveness. All of us must come to God and repent for our deeds, thoughts, and dispositions that are contrary to His will. We need the cleansing blood of Jesus to be applied to our lives daily. Our ability to be forgiven hinges on our ability to forgive others. Thus, I must always humble myself before God and ask that His blood be applied to my life, so that I am cleansed from all of my sin. And just as I desire the Lord to forgive me, I must also forgive others. My ability to be forgiven is contingent upon my ability to forgive. Many people are walking around with years of unforgiven sin because they are still harboring revenge, bitterness and a lack of forgiveness in their heart for others. King David says, *"Hide thy face from my sins, and blot out all mine iniquities. Create in me a clean heart, O God; and renew a right spirit within me"* **(Psalms 51:9-10)**. This must be the demeanor and attitude of all children of God. When we are cleansed from our sins, we are free from accusation on the part of Satan, and are able to experience the width and depth of the power that comes from being in a healthy relationship with God.

Finally, Jesus admonishes us to ask the Father for strength and deliverance from the evil one. Asking God to allow us to overcome the temptations and traps of the enemy is of utmost importance. We need God to grant us favor and mercy in our daily lives so that we can have the victory over the enemy and our character flaws. When God leads us, we are assured of the victory. When God is absent, we are destined for defeat. The doxology of worship to God is the seal of our prayers. It says to God that you believe He will do all He said He would do, and that you trust Him as the all mighty God of the universe. He has all the power. He only elicits all the glory in the universe. And since He is the only Eternal God, His praises shall be made and given by His creation forever and ever.

PRAYING IN THE SPIRIT AND OTHER ASPECTS OF PRAYER

Paul encouraged the Corinthian Church to pray with the spirit and understanding. I **Corinthians 14:15** says, *"What is it then? I will pray with the spirit, and I will pray with the understanding also: I will sing with the spirit and I will sing with the understanding also."* This passage of scripture is powerful and quite clear. Praying in the spirit means praying under the influence and direction of the spirit. There has been gross misunderstanding and misuse of tongues in the Body of Christ. Through the spirit of error, many leaders have led their members to believe that they are engaged in spiritual warfare when speaking in tongues. This is directly untrue, but indirectly true. I say directly untrue because the believer is not hurting the enemy directly when they speak in tongues. I say indirectly true, because the believer is strengthening them self for spiritual warfare when they are speaking in tongues. Paul made it plain that the only spiritual warfare taking place when we speak in tongues is the internal war within ourselves. Therefore, speaking in tongues is an important element of prayer, because the believer is able to strengthen themselves in the Holy Ghost. There is a great need to edify one's self before engaging in offensive spiritual warfare. However, we should not think that the enemy gets nervous or is even fazed by a bunch of believers running around a church speaking in tongues. Satan's kingdom is only threatened when believers use speaking in tongues to strengthen themselves for warfare and begin speaking and releasing those mysteries into the earth realm. Until we seek for understanding, those mysteries remain of non-effect in the life of other believers.

There are other aspects of prayer that should be examined. We are admonished to pray for the sick *"Is any sick among you? Let him call for the elders of the church; and let them pray over him, anointing him with oil in the name of the Lord"* **(James 5:14)**, and pray without vain repetition, *"But when ye pray, use not vain repetitions, as the heathen do: for they think that they shall be heard for their much speaking"* **(Matthew**

6:7). Prayers can become memorials before God, "*And when he looked on him, he was afraid, and said, What is it, Lord? And he said unto him, Thy prayers and thine alms are come up for a memorial before God*" (Acts 10:4), are kept in golden vials in the form of odors (*And when he had taken the book, the four beasts and four and twenty elders fell down before the Lamb, having every one of them harps, and golden vials full of odours, which are the prayers of saints*" (Revelation 5:8), are a part of Christian fellowship "*And they continued steadfastly in the apostles' doctrine and fellowship, and in breaking of bread, and in prayers*" (Acts 2:42), can set captives free, "*Peter therefore was kept in prison: but prayer was made without ceasing of the church unto God for him*" (Acts 12:5), and when given by the righteous, prayer produces results "*Confess your faults one to another, and pray one for another, that ye may be healed. The effectual fervent prayer of a righteous man availeth much*" (James 5:16). Besides making petitions, prayer is the means by which we develop a relationship with God. Through prayer we have the privilege of casting our cares upon the Lord, "*Casting all your care upon him; for he careth for you*" (1 Peter 5:7), and the privilege of receiving guidance and direction from God. The devil hates a saint who has developed a relationship with their God. There is a very popular saying, "Much prayer, much power; little prayer, little power."

When we enter into prayer, we must have a submissive spirit. We must allow the spirit to guide us in our prayer life. Most of the time, we have no understanding about what we should pray for or how we should pray. We are limited in knowledge, understanding and life experience, and therefore must depend on the Lord to help us pray. What an awesome God we serve. We serve a God that will give us the words to speak to Him in order to release heaven's power on our behalf. **Romans 8:26** says, *"Likewise the Spirit also helpeth our infirmities: for we know not what we should ray for as we ought: but the Spirit itself maketh intercession for us with groanings which cannot be uttered."* There are issues in your spirit that have not been revealed to you. There are some attacks that Satan has planned against you that you won't know about unless God reveals them to you. When you pray as the Holy Spirit gives you the utterance, you will begin to pray according to the will of God which will make you an effective and efficient prayer warrior. International, national, and local government issues will begin to enter into your prayers without you planning them to. Issues concerning family, associates and even people you have never met will be expressed in your prayer time when you allow the Holy Spirit to give you utterance. It requires a very submissive spirit on the part of the believer in order to engage in this level of warfare, but it must be the passion and desire of the believer to enter into this level. For it is in this level of prayer that the power of God will be made manifest in the lives of people.

INTERCESSORY PRAYER

To discuss the power of intercessory pray, I will begin by quoting Evangelist Lottie Stearne from her book *Treasure in the Midst of Ruins-Birth out of Bondage*. Concerning a very difficult time in her life she writes, *"God filled my mother with the Holy Ghost in 1975. This was a very crucial time in my life. God knew that the only thing that would keep me from being consumed by the devil was to have someone directly related to me to pray without ceasing...My mother's prayers began to cover me and even unto this very day I know that is why I was not destroyed by the adversary"*[14] *pg. 31*. Intercessory prayer is another aspect of the powerful weapon of prayer. Sometimes called "gap dwelling", intercessory pray is when the believer begins warring in the spirit for issues and people in a fervent manner. Now that you understand that the real battle is not with what we see, but the unseen kingdom of Satan which is only manifested in the lives of people, situations and social systems, you can begin to move in intercessory pray. When engaging in intercessory prayer, we put our needs aside and begin to war on the behalf of others. Thus, the word of God must be used in this level of prayer, because God's will must be done in order for people and entities to reap the benefit of intercessory pray. God is seeking for "gap dwellers" that are willing to get outside of themselves and wage war against the enemy.

Ezekiel 22:30 says, *"And I sought for a man among*

---

[14] Stearne, Lottie. "Treasure in the Midst of Ruins-Birth out of Bondage". AuthorHouse (2009) Bloomington, IN

them, that should make up the hedge, and stand in the gap before me for the land, that I should not destroy it: but I found none." God says that He was looking for **"someone."** Please note the suggestion here. God didn't need a thousand people. He didn't even need one hundred. He was simply looking for "some-ONE". Then we see what He wanted them to do. First, He wanted them to "make up the hedges". He wanted someone to begin to rebuild the broken places that are originally designed to protect and insulate people. When we engage in intercessory prayer, we are rebuilding things that will have life-long effects in the lives of people. We rebuild homes, relationships, cities and even nations through intercessory prayer.

Being active in the political process and in community affairs is extremely important, but prayer is the key element to seeing godly results in any of the issues facing man. **Psalms 127:1** says, *"Except the Lord build the house, they labour in vain that build it: except the Lord keep the city, the watchman waketh but in vain."* Your intercessory prayer will begin to build the hedges that will protect people, communities and nations from the winds that Satan is blowing. The Lord answers three questions that anyone engaged in prayers needs to have answered. He tells the people of Ezekiel's day very clearly to *"stand in the gap before him for the land"* (Ezekiel 22:30). Where do we stand? We stand in the gap. How do we stand? We stand before him. Why do we stand? We stand for the land.

The reason we stand in the gap is because it is the gaps

within the lives of people and our cities that are defenseless against the attacks of the enemy. Our prayers make up the difference in the lives of people. Job had children who were riotous and not always doing what God willed for them to do. Along with trying to raise his children in the fear of the Lord, Job also interceded for his children through sacrifices and offerings. **Job 1:4-5** says, *"And his sons went and feasted in their houses, everyone his day: and sent and called for their three sisters to eat and to drink with them. And it was so, when the days of their feasting were gone about, that Job sent and sanctified them, and rose up early in the morning, and offered burnt offerings according to the number of them all: for Job said, It may be that my sons have sinned, and cursed God in the hearts. Thus did Job continually."* Note that intercessory prayer is a full time job. There are so many issues facing humanity, that the warfare waged against the enemy's kingdom must be continual and consistent. God honors the prayers of the righteous. When we enter into intercessory prayer, we are connected with the full width and depth of the Kingdom of God which includes all beings in heaven and earth.

Then the Lord says that when we stand in the gap that we must stand *"before Him"*. We present our prayers unto the Lord daily and without ceasing. But please note that the phrase, *before him* has a much greater implication than just standing in front of God. In order to stand before Him, we must first have access to Him. Access has been provided for us through the blood of Jesus, but we only access this liberty by virtue of using the blood to keep ourselves clean in the sight of the Lord. This is why repentance and walking in reverence of the Lord is so important. You don't want your access to God blocked by sin or any other entanglements that may hinder you from being an effective intercessor. **Hebrews 4:16** says, *"Let us therefore come boldly unto the throne of grace that we may obtain mercy, and find grace to help in time of need."* In order to be able to be effective in prayer and enter into the throne room of God, we must operate in the spirit of holiness and humility. Then when we access the throne room, everything we ask for will be freely given to us and the enemy will have to leave out of any situation we cast him out of.

Remember, **James** says in **chapter 5** verse **16**, *"Confess your faults one to another, and pray one for another, that ye may be healed. The effectual fervent prayer of the righteous man availeth much."* Note the connection between sins and our effectiveness. When sin is high in our lives, we won't be effective prayer warriors, but when we have come to God and made our hands clean from sin and shame, we will be powerful prayer warriors that the devil cannot stop. Our prayers are so powerful, that they can affect change in areas and regions that we may not even have physical access to. This explains why God was looking for someone to stand in the gap **"for the land."** Our prayers should not be restricted to just our families and our ministries. Rather, our prayers must encompass a wide range of issues that are saturated in the human crisis. We should pray for international leaders, national leaders, local leaders, church leaders, people we work with, things we see on the news or read about in the paper, family members and anyone or anything else that the Holy Spirit leads us to pray for. We may not always see the results of our prayers, but must have faith that God is working things out in these issues.

When you are praying in the spirit, God will lead you to pray for individuals who may be in trouble or in need of strengthening in a specific area of their life. By you praying on their behalf, God will squash the plans of the enemy. If you don't fill the gap, they could be lost. Your prayer could be the only power between life and death for your loved ones! Therefore, it is vital that you be very sensitive to the voice of the Holy Spirit. A gap is an open avenue by which the enemy can come in like a flood. Therefore, we must fill these gaps with spiritual warfare.

Ephesians 4:27 says, *"Neither give place to the devil."* The scripture here is referring to openings of dissention and conflict that happen when we don't seek reconciliation in our personal relationships. Yet, I believe we can use this same concept for our discussion. We should not allow the devil to have a foot hole, or opening into the areas that have been claimed for God's kingdom. We must be aggressive in our prayers, demanding strongholds to be broken, yokes to be destroyed and chains to be loosened. Someone who is bound by the spirit of oppression may not be able to free himself. However, we who are free by the spirit of God have the power to release them and take dominion over all of the enemy's weapons. **Luke 9:1** says, *"Then he called his twelve disciples together, and gave them power* *and authority over all devils, and to cure diseases."* God will use your prayers to stop car accidents, heal people, deliver people out of bad relationships and situations and bring the glory of God in the Body of Christ so that souls will be saved and set free.

The devil wants us to be so self consumed with our personal issues, that we never begin to engage in warfare on behalf of someone or something outside of our self. The devil also wants us to be people who complain about issues and gossip about people, but never move in the spirit to intercede for them. I have encountered countless Christians who choose to talk, discuss, and complain about issues as opposed to praying. It is easy to sit outside of the situations that face so many and analyze the wrong and the rights of it. People often feel free to express their criticisms to the world concerning issues and situations that are not directly tied to themselves. The intercessory prayer warriors are different. The real intercessory prayer warrior is one who prays immediately after having heard some bad news concerning someone. The intercessory prayer warrior is tied emotionally (God's emotion) to people, circumstances and world realities through the power of the Holy Ghost. Thus, they always have a mind to pray for God's mercy, grace and intervention in the lives of men.

FASTING

Fasting is an absolute must if the believer is going to fulfill their potential as a tool for spiritual warfare. If the tool is tainted with the desires of this world it won't be effective against the devil and his minions. *Fast* simply means to go without. Fasting removes the most basic need of human existence which causes an increased reliance on God to provide and sustain. Many types of fasts have been promoted in Christendom. Some have promoted fasts from fruit, meat, television, and other types of fasts that focus on removing something people desire from their daily routine. Some have come up with very creative names for various fasts which highlight certain incidents in scripture. These fasts have probably become popular because of how busy people are in today's society and their inability to manage both their spiritual and natural involvements. However, the Spirit of the Lord has directed me to only endorse a strict traditional fast in which the believer abstains from all food, water and all forms of entertainment. Some believers have medical conditions which require them to take medicine with food or require them to have a certain level of nutritional intake each day. In these cases, the believer should follow the directions of their physician through prayer.

Fasting gives the believer victory over the world. When the Bible discusses the world, it is dealing with the "cosmos" or world systems. All world systems are an expression of the ideas and deficiencies of fallen man and are in and of themselves anti-God. It is not to suggest that there can be no good to come from various world systems, but it is to acknowledge that the systems of this world are not created by man to give glory to God. The systems of this world are created to be self existent and independent of the eternal God. Thus, the believer must gain victory over the world in order to engage in spiritual warfare and please God.

THE WORLD

John says in **1 John 2:15**, *"Love not the world, neither the things that are in the world. If any man love the world, the love of the Father is not in him."* Fasting stands against man's natural desire to love the world and the things that are in the world. Please note that John says, "Love NOT". In other words, there should be no ties to anything in this life. It is amazing that many who claim to have spiritual depth, seem to be so taken and attached to things of this life such as cars, clothes and houses. Many of them even expound the idea that "prosperity" is the will of God. Yet, this quest for worldly goods, esteem and power is in direct contradiction to John's assertion here. "Love NOT the world". Since it is natural (in my flesh) to desire the things of this life more than I desire the things of God, I must do something to help destroy this innate desire. Also, note that John points out that it is impossible for a person who loves the world to also have the love of the Father in him. It takes the love, desires, and motives of the Father in order to have the correct priorities as it pertains to life and spirituality. Without the love of the Father, one will live unto himself and become a wasteland of self indulgent behaviors that are against the Kingdom of God. This is where fasting comes in. Fasting creates a reliance on God and allows for His love to dwell on the inside of you, which becomes the fuel by which faith and strength work together against the kingdom of Satan.

THE SELF

Fasting will help destroy three basic desires that will stand in conflict with the will of God; lust in the body, ungodly desires, and any quest for esteem and power. This topic was covered earlier in the book but deserves further consideration. Fasting must be done with purpose and the purpose is to destroy these three basic desires. John continues his discourse in 1 John saying, *"For all that is in the world, the lust of the flesh, and the lust of the eyes, and the pride of life, is not of the Father, but is of the world"* (1 John 2:16). The key here is that John recognizes that these three elements are "all that is in the world". As complex as the world is, it is actually made of very basic desires, which if addressed, can be brought under control by the believer. Eve was not able to win the victory over these basic desires. Genesis 3 shows the power of these very basic needs when Moses records the fall. **Genesis 3:6,** *"And when the woman saw that the tree was* **good** *for food, and that it was* **pleasant to the eyes,** *and a tree to be desired to* **make one wise,** *she took of the fruit thereof, and did eat, and gave also unto her husband with her; and he did eat".* Satan planted the seed of suggestion, but it was these three basic lusts that caused her to be deceived. Satan's desire was to subvert the authority that God had vested into man, thereby allowing Satan to rule earth due to man's default.

[227]

THE ENEMY

Jesus won the victory over these three lusts when He was tempted in the wilderness. Matthew's gospel records that after Jesus had been tempted and fasting for forty days and forty nights, Satan confronted Him in three major human areas. The enemy knew Jesus was very hungry. Satan assumed while in that state he would be able to get the victory over Him. What he didn't understand is that the stripping of the flesh actually makes one stronger spiritually, because the individual's reliance is solely on God. Jesus won the victory over the lust of the flesh when He was tempted to turn stones into bread. He won the victory over the pride of life and vain glory. Lastly, He won the victory over the lust of the eye when He was tempted with all of the kingdoms of the world. Satan made a proposal to Jesus that would allow Jesus to gain all of the kingdoms of the world outside of the plan of God. It was the denying of the flesh that allowed Jesus to stand strong against the enemy. No Christian can stand against the enemy without a life of fasting.

The enemy understands that it is impossible to wage warfare against him without a life of fasting. Anyone claiming to move in a deep level of prophesy, evangelism, or the gifts, and does not have a life of fasting and prayer, is deceived and is probably operating in rebellion or under some spirit of darkness. The flesh must be crucified in order to hear from God and have the power over spiritual wickedness. A Christian can live a mediocre life in Christ without fasting, but will never move into the deeper things of God and warfare without fasting. Joel cried these words, *"Blow the trumpet in Zion, sanctify a fast, call a solemn assembly.* **Joel 2:15.** God instructed Joel to declare a fast by blowing a trumpet. The trumpet was a tool used in Israel to let the people know a proclamation was about to be made and to declare war with the expectation of victory. The trumpet had to be blown loud to get the attention of everyone in the Kingdom. Note that the trumpet here comes before the directions to "sanctify" a fast. The fast was set aside for a specific purpose in which only the people of God were invited to partake. When God is about to shift the plight of His people, He will often prompt the leaders to call a fast. Satan will always try to block the Body from engaging in fasting. But reader, God will also use you to sanctify for yourself, family, and community a fast that will have long term effects.

When God wants to empower his people, He will use a fast to get them ready for the blessings that are about to be released. Fasting, being a basic and pertinent sacrifice necessary for victory, frees the believer to receive from God. In the book of **1 Corinthians 2:4** it states, *"The carnal man cannot receive the things of God because they are spiritually discerned".* A man who is walking and living in the flesh (according to the laws of the natural realm) cannot perceive or receive the things of God. Because God's thoughts are above our thoughts and His ways are above our ways, we must be moved to a higher spiritual state in order to attain His mind. It is the power of God's mind and directive that

[229]

allows us to wage warfare against the enemy and defeat him in the earth realm.

COMMITMENT AND FOCUS

Due to the "quick fix", "microwave" spirit that we currently live in, many believers don't know how to wait patiently on the Lord and travail before God. It takes focus and patience to seek the face (will) of God. Some very popular preachers have even made fun of the child of God who would go to an altar and cry out before the Lord. I have even witnessed people removed out of church because they were at the altar praying at the wrong time. The house of God should be a place where people can lay before God and seek His face. It may take hours, days, or even months to seek the face of God. The popularized two and three day revivals may not be enough. A one to two hour service may not be enough. Believer, you have to be willing to seek God's face for as long as it takes. I have witnessed television evangelist looking at the television screen while praying, as if to suggest some depth in God that doesn't require any focus or travail in the spirit. Yet, the Bible only gives examples of men and women who knew that in order to receive from God, there must be a removal of the self and a stripping away of the carnality. Even in the world, when people want to solicit the attention of their government, they will fast. They will go on a fast to save a park, or an animal, or to express their disapproval of a government action. If people in the world sacrifice and fast for things they believe in, why wouldn't you make fasting a vital part of your life in order to get God to move on your behalf? Fasting is God's mandate for the children of God. When we fast, God gives us His attention and our flesh is put under subjection.

In Daniel, Daniel gives us a good example of the power of fasting. In **Daniel 9:2-3** it states, *"In the first year of his reign I Daniel understood by books the number of the years, whereof the word of the LORD came to Jeremiah the prophet, that he would accomplish seventy years in the desolations of Jerusalem. And I set my face unto the Lord God, to seek by prayer and supplications, with fasting, and sackcloth, and ashes."* Fasting must be used by the child of God to "set their face to God". That means that above and beyond the benefits of putting the flesh under subjection and gaining spiritual strength, fasting is also used when there is a serious and heavy burden in the earth realm that needs to be lifted. All things in the natural have spiritual foundations, and the believer must use fasting as a tool to understand the mind of God concerning secular and Kingdom issues. Daniel set his face to God with a broken spirit, prayer, supplication, fasting, sackcloth and ashes.

This type of intent is the same intent we see when Enoch walked with God (Genesis 6), Noah built for God (Genesis 8), Abraham moved for God (Genesis 12), and Jacob wrestled with God (Genesis 35). It is prayer and fasting with purpose. It is a level of focus and dedication that goes past the normal everyday spiritual things we do as believers. This type of focus should not only be the response to traumatic or severe situations, but for daily empowerment. Focus, dedication and discipline should become a way of life for us, so that we are always ready for negative situations when they arise. Daniel was determined to hear from God and understand God's secrets; we must also.

Daniel's fasting was honored by heaven. His focus and dedication caused him to get a response from heaven that all believers have the ability to receive. **Daniel 9: 21-22** states, *"Yea, whiles I was speaking in prayer, even the man Gabriel, whom I had seen in the vision at the beginning, being caused to fly swiftly, touched me about the time of the evening oblation. And he informed me, and talked with me, and said, O Daniel, I am now come forth to give thee skill and understanding."* Daniel's fasting and prayer was the catalyst to make Gabriel fly swiftly. Angels move swiftly on behalf of the fasting believer. Note also, that Gabriel showed up to give Daniel skill and understanding. If we are going to fight this war, we must have skill and understanding. This is what fasting gives the believer. Fasting gives us the ability to exist outside of the world systems for knowledge, and stand with power and authority in God's Kingdom. God will release all of heaven's resources on your behalf when you fast. When we give up our resources of energy and strength, heaven releases its resources of energy and strength to destroy Satan's kingdom.

Fasting also assures victory against the highest and strongest demonic forces. **Mark 9:17-29** records a story in which a man brought his demon possessed son to the disciples to have the demon cast out. The disciples didn't have the power to cast out the demon. This demon was extremely strong, seen in its ability to hold the child captive against the father's will and cause the child to engage in multiple demonic expressions such as depression, a lack of speech, inability to hear, violent spells, unexplained sickness expressed by foaming, sporadic behaviors, and suicide attempts through fire and water. Mark records the private concern of the disciples and Jesus' response to their concern. *Verse 28-29 says, "And when he was come into the house, his disciples asked him privately, "Why could not we cast him out?" And he said unto them, "This kind can come forth by nothing, but by prayer and fasting".*

There are some demons and spiritual wickedness that will only be defeated by prayer and fasting. Not prayer alone, but prayer and fasting. During the greatest battles of one's life, is when they must use the greatest weapons in their arsenal. Fasting is one of those weapons that will strengthen the believer, give greater discernment, fill one with revelation, give victory over the world, give greater authority, bring clarity to the word of God, and cause the enemy to respond to a believer's words according to the will of God.

MEDITATION

Meditation is very powerful in keeping your spiritual man "tuned-up" and focused on the things of God. Very few believers have tapped into the power of meditation because

[233]

it has been considered weird or humanistic because of the use of it in religions such as Buddhism, Hinduism and meditative forms such as yoga. Yet, meditation is a foundation of spirituality that has been sanctioned by God. It is God who desires for His children to focus their energies and mind on His will, His way, and His precepts.

King David understood the power of meditation in **Psalms 1:1** stating, *"...But his delight is in the law of the Lord; and in his law doth he meditate day and night."* David is referring here to what he describes as a blessed man; a man that is able to remove himself from evil and to stand in the midst of wicked world. The law of the Lord or the word of God is the focus of all Christian meditation. There are two prominent words used for meditate in the Old Testament *Hagah* and *Siyach*. These words collectively mean to murmur, ponder, and to converse with. The most unique of these definitions is to "converse with". The idea of meditation as a conversation is powerful in that it focuses on the exchange that takes place. I give my thoughts to God and He validates, reproves, or removes those thoughts with His thoughts. David goes on to say in the fifteenth Psalm of Instruction, **Psalms 77:12**, *"I will meditate also of all thy work, and talk of thy doings."* Look at the connection. When we meditate, then we have the power to speak. Our words have authority, based on meditation. Think of a rotisserie griller where the meat is turned over and over again to insure that it is cooked to perfection and that all the seasoning permeates throughout. This is the way God's word should permeate the believer. As the believer meditates, God will begin to download and reveal truths of His Word, current political and social affairs and internal issues that are specific to the deliverance and empowerment of the believer. Paul encourages Timothy concerning the power of meditation and profit that comes from focusing. **1Timothy 4:15** says, *"Meditate upon these things; give thyself wholly to them; that thy profiting may appear to all."*

When we meditate and give ourselves wholly to what God has commanded, we will experience profit. God causes us to grow through His word which gives us insight into how to engage in warfare. **Amos 3:7** says, *"Surely the Lord God will do nothing, but he revealeth his secret unto his servants the prophets."* When the believer is walking in revelation, the enemy cannot gain the upper hand in warfare. There will be no surprises that will catch the meditating believer off guard.

Discussions, Reflections, and Activities

1. Discuss ways in which your personal prayer time can be improved. What do you need to do in order to make these improvements?

2. Discuss ways in which prayer can be improved and promoted at your local church. How can you encourage a church movement for more effective prayer?

[235]

3. The Prayer List: Prayer lists are very common. Develop a prayer list that includes the categories below and use it as a guide for one week. As people and entities need to be included or removed, make the appropriate adjustments to it.

Prayer List (These categories are not in any specific order)

Personal	Relatives	The Unsaved
Forgiveness	Community Issues	Personal Ministry
Lord I Praise you because…	Regional Issues	Enemies
Spiritual Leadership	National Issues	Others
Local Issues	World Issues	Less Fortunate

4. Meditation: As a group or alone, choose a passage of scripture (preferably from Psalms, Proverbs, or words of Christ). Read it out loud to the group or to yourself,

[236]

and take five minutes to meditate on the passage. After your time of meditation, discuss your thoughts with a small group. This is not a time for interpretation, but reflective meditation and expressive illumination. There are no wrong answers.

Notes:

_____

_____

_____

_____

_____

_____

_____

_____

_____

_____

_____

_____

_____

_____

_____

_____

_____

_____

_____

"Wherefore hath God also highly exalted him, and given him a name which is above every name."

Philippians 2:9

Chapter 11

THE NAME OF JESUS

One of the most powerful revelations of spiritual warfare is the knowledge that Jesus is the supreme name of the universe, because it is the name of God. It will take another literary work to do this subject the justice it deserves, but I will give you just enough to begin using the name of Jesus with power and authority. When a believer declares to do something in the "Name of Jesus", what they are saying is that they are operating under the direct authority of Jesus. To operate under that authority means that whatever power He has, you have been given access to

[238]

by virtue of your relationship with Him. Jesus means *Jehovah is Salvation*. It is the same name of Joshua in the Old Testament. For an extended study, look at the similarities between Joshua and Jesus. The children of Israel knew God as Jehovah which is translated *Lord* along with a description of the action God had taken on their behalf. In *Names of God*, Nathan Stone does a wonderful job of giving an in-depth study of the names given to God in the Old Testament. In his introduction he states, *"It has been the writer's purpose to show not only the significance of the names of God in the Old Testament, but that they find their complement and fulfillment in the person and work of the Lord Jesus Christ in the New—he who is the effulgence of the glory and the image of the substance of Jehovah, and in whom "dwelleth all the fullness of the Godhead bodily"* [15]*pg. 5*. I appreciate Nathan Stone's illumination concerning the foreshadowing of names in the Old Testament which points to the fullness of God's divine name and personification; Jesus. The only correction I would make to Nathan Stone's assessment is that what he is calling "names of God" in the Old Testament is actually descriptive titles which are all encompassed underneath the name of Jesus. When I say "Jesus", there is no need to call on any of the other descriptive titles encompassed by His character and actions. This understanding is the very foundation by which the believer now stands in to make declarations of authority through the name of Jesus.

---

[15]Stone, Nathan. "Names of God". The Moody Bible Institute (1944). Chicago, IL

Thus, God was called Jehovah Jireh (The Lord that forsees the need and provides), Jehovah Shalom (The Lord of Peace), and Jehovah Ropheh (The Lord that Heals) to name a few. He was also called Advocate (1 John 2:1), Almighty (Rev. 1:8; Mt. 28:18), Alpha and Omega (Rev. 1:8; 22:13), Atoning Sacrifice for our Sins (1 John 2:2), Author of Salvation (Heb. 2:10), Bridegroom (Mt. 9:15), Creator (John 1:3), Eternal Life (1 John 1:2; 5:20), Gate (John 10:9), Firstborn From the Dead (Rev. 1:5), Holy and True (Rev. 3:7), King Eternal (1 Tim. 1:17), Lamb of God (John 1:29), Lion of the Tribe of Judah(Rev.5:5),Mighty God (Isa. 9:6), Our Great God and Savior (Titus 2:13), Resurrection and Life (John 11:25), True Light (John 1:9), Truth (John 1:14; 14:6), Way (John 14:6), Wisdom of God (1 Cor. 1:24), Word (John 1:1)[16], and a whole host of other descriptive titles and names that magnify all of the wonderful qualities and power of our wonderful savior. Some would say that God has a lot of names, but the truth is that God has been "called" a lot of names. He only ascribed one name to Himself. When it came time for God to give His son (son being Himself in flesh), He left no room for confusion concerning what to called His gift to humanity. God specifically told Mary that the child she would be bearing would be named Jesus. Obviously He told her to name the child Jesus because that is the name of God and it is through that name that the blessings of the new covenant are made manifest (Matthew 1:21). Therefore, Jesus is the only name (authority) given on earth that has the power to defuse and destroy the kingdom of Satan.

---

[16] www.jesuschristis.com (2009)

It is very important for believers to understand that Jesus is the name of God, because Jesus is God. Isaiah looked through His prophetic lenses and declared, *"Therefore the Lord himself shall give you a sign; Behold, a virgin shall conceive, and bear a son, and shall call his name Immanuel"* (Isaiah 7:14). The name Immanuel means God with us. Yes, God with us. Not just a prophet or a good family member, but God Himself. Again, Isaiah receives the revelation of the power and person of Jesus when he states, *"For unto us a child is born, unto us a son is given: and the government shall be upon his shoulder: and his name shall be called Wonderful, Counsellor,* **The mighty God,** **The everlasting Father,** *The Prince of Peace"* (Isaiah 9: 6). Jesus is the mighty God and the everlasting Father, and yes, He is also the Prince. Although, *mighty God, Wonderful* and *everlasting Father* are all descriptions of His person, His actual name is Jesus.

Satan hates the name of Jesus. Jesus showed His power over Satan by undoing the works of Satan. Satan, who was Lucifer, lost his place and position with God by trying to exalt his throne. He did not understand that his throne could not be exalted because the exalted throne was reserved for and is now occupied by our Lord and Savior Jesus Christ. Satan's dismal defeat in the wilderness, at Calvary, in Hell, and in the Resurrection proved to him that he would always be but a footnote in the literary work of the Author and Finisher of our faith, Jesus.

Remember when Moses wanted to see the glory of God? What did God tell Moses? He said, "*... I will make all my goodness pass before thee,* **and I will proclaim the name of the LORD (Jehovah) before thee;** *and will be gracious to whom I will be gracious, and will shew mercy on whom I will shew mercy*" **(Exodus 33:19).** To know the name of the Lord is a sign of fellowship, intimacy, and power with God. God revealed His name to the world when Gabriel made his announcement to Mary. *"And she shall bring forth a son, and thou shalt call his name JESUS: for he shall save his people from their sins"* **(Matthew 1:21).** When we use the name of Jesus, all demons have to cease activity and yield to His power. Jesus has all power and has given us His name in order to subdue the enemy and his kingdom. The different systems by which believers perceive God are often given much debate. "Is God one entity in essence?" Is God three persons operating as one? Is God simply beyond our ability to perceive? These are all the sentiments of believers around the world. This is understandable, because as stated before, *"...great is the mystery of godliness: God was manifest in flesh..."* **(1 Timothy 3:16).** Understanding the essence of God is truly a revelation that must be received. However, no matter what your doctrinal view of God is, whether Oneness, Trinitarian or some other perspective, one thing is sure, the name of Jesus speaks to the power and person of the Almighty God. In all systems that attempt to explain the essence of God, the name of Jesus is consistent in them all. This is why we pray in His name, baptize in His name, praise His name, worship His name, and do all things in His name **(Colossians 3: 17).**

The name of Jesus speaks to His power in creation and His ultimate authority over all creation. The Bible says in **Phillipians 2:9**, *"Wherefore hath God also highly exalted him, and given him a name which is above every name."* Then in **Colossians 1:16** *"For by him were all things created, that are in heaven, and that are in earth, visible and invisible, whether [they be] thrones, or dominions, or principalities, or powers: all things were created by him, and for him."* The immutable power of Jesus is seen in the creation and the purpose of all life. His name is above every name, not only because of what He accomplished in His death, resurrection and ascension, but also due to His power in all creation as creator. Note here that all creation exists because of Him, by Him and for Him. That means that He is ultimately the last say and authority on all things in creation. His name is above principalities, dominions, and thrones, both seen and unseen. The trees are created for His glory. The unseen matter that we can't see is for His glory. The angels are created for His glory. The name of Jesus is so powerful that all of creation will bow to it and Him. Even the demons in Hell, Satan and his kingdom will bow to the name of Jesus. The name of Jesus causes things to be created. It causes the atmosphere, environment, spirits and all things tangible and intangible to stand at attention to the will of God. Therefore, when we call on the name of Jesus, we are calling on the greatest authority in the universe. He bears the name, because He is God manifested in the flesh.

There can be no victory in spiritual warfare without proper use of the name of Jesus. Jesus sent His disciples out

[243]

to conduct ministry in His name. Luke records the victory that these disciples experienced. *"And the seventy returned again with joy, saying, Lord, even the devils are subject unto us through thy name"* (Luke 10:17). These disciples were able to cast out and subdue devils by using the name of Jesus. These disciples had not experienced the infilling of the Holy Spirit yet, which meant they were performing these works because of their relationship with Jesus and use of His name. When He sent them out, He sent them out with His authority. The name of Jesus should be used by all believers when entering into spiritual warfare. Paul goes even further and says, *"And whatsoever ye do in word or deed, [do] all in the name of the Lord Jesus, giving thanks to God and the Father by him"* (Colossians 3:17).

BINDING AND LOOSING

The scriptural understanding of binding and loosing is found in two distinct uses. The first is to establish God's will, policy, law, or precedent in the earth realm on behalf of the Kingdom of God. The second is the ability to restrict, tie, or diffuse the works of Satan. Essentially, binding and loosing can be reworded as "restricting" and "releasing". These two modes of binding and loosing are extremely powerful and can be very effective in engaging in spiritual warfare.

First, this weapon of binding and loosing has been extrapolated from the words of Jesus when he spoke to Peter concerning the opening of the Kingdom of God. He stated,

"And I will give unto thee the keys of the kingdom of heaven: and whatsoever thou shalt bind on earth shall be bound in heaven: and whatsoever thou shalt loose on earth shall be loosed in heaven" (Matthew 16:19). Peter was given keys, which represent the authority to open. This authority was given both by Jesus' words here, but also confirmed by the infilling of the Holy Spirit that all the believers received on the day of Pentecost. Peter was given the mantle to be the mouthpiece and authority in the earth realm concerning what God's perfect will was concerning salvation, life, and the Church. The text may be better read as, *"Whatsoever is loosed in heaven can be loosed in earth"*. Thus, Peter was not acting according to his own will or thoughts, but under the unction and authority of God. On the day of Pentecost, Peter preached the first message of the Church which led 3000 souls to salvation. He bound the lies that they were deceived by, and loosed the truth of the gospel. Reader, God does not sanction man to make random decisions concerning the Kingdom. Teachings that assert that the believer can speak and desire whatever they want and God will endorse them are false doctrines. All things must be according to the will of God, and when they are, the power of God will be released on behalf of the Kingdom. We will then have the power to bind and loose the initiatives and policies of the Kingdom in the earth realm.

This idea of God's will is clearly seen in what is called the Lord's Prayer (Once again, it is actually the disciple's prayer). *"Thy kingdom come. Thy will be done in earth, as it is in heaven"* (Matthew 6:10). Note that the Kingdom is beckoned to come. The issues and entities that need to be changed are not in heaven, but they are in the earth realm. Power is only released when God's Kingdom is established in the earth, not man's ideas or ambitions. Therefore, when an individual moves into binding spiritual wickedness, rulers of darkness, powers, and principalities, there must be a sanctioning from the Kingdom first. This is because no man, no matter what his position or title is in the local church, has the power to bind spiritual wickedness. It takes the power of God to bind the devil, which means that one must walk according to the will and desires of God before they can be used to bind the devil. God says, *"...not by might, nor by power, but by my spirit, saith the Lord of hosts"* **(Zechariah 4:6).** God is the warrior, and we are the tools God has decided to use to make weapons of war. The believer must not forget this, because to err in this knowledge can mean life or death. Satan would love for a believer to walk in self pride and false strength; attempting to do a spiritual thing in their natural strength.

Jesus dispatches the power of restricting and releasing to the apostles as a dimension of their ambassadorship in the earth realm. He gives the apostles the power to bind or loose someone's guilt or innocence in social matters through the witness of two or three. Concerning someone who has trespassed against a member of the church, Jesus says, *"And if he shall neglect to hear them, tell it unto the church: but if he neglect to hear the church, let him be unto thee as an heathen man and a publican. Verily I say unto you, whatsoever ye shall bind on earth shall be bound in heaven: and whatsoever ye shall loose on earth shall be loosed in heaven"* **(Matthew 18:17-18).** In both the former and latter cases in this section, the binding and loosing directive is used in the context of taking control of situations and establishing a precedent or policy by which God will honor. Thus, binding and loosing allows the believer to establish a new precedent in the earth realm that can be an example for what God thinks about an issue or matter. This power is often used by a pastor who establishes a policy rule for his or her church. Members might question the policy because there may not be an explicit law in scripture for its precedence. But the pastor has been given the power to bind and loose in the earth realm and God will stand by the policy decisions of leadership that are consistent with His will. As ambassadors of the Kingdom of God, we have a duty and right to establish His will and way in the earth realm. Thus, binding and loosing is the act of restricting or liberating ideas and entities in the earth realm by the authority of God.

The second type of binding and loosing available to the believer is one that is much more highlighted within Christian circles. I see many preachers at services and on television claiming that they are going to bind the devil and loose some type of blessing or virtue. It has made the power of binding and loosing seem accessible to anyone who believes anything. People are ultimately hurt in faith and life by the lies told by many leaders who have claimed to bind something on behalf of the believer, even though there were no results to substantiate that a binding did in fact take place. The believer leaves away thinking that whatever they were struggling with has been bound, just to find out that it is still active and sometimes even stronger. The word bind in Greek is *"deo"* which means to *knit, tie, wind, put under obligation, bring into law, forbid, stop or prohibit.* Therefore, other than the literal use of the word which is to actually put one in chains, when the Bible speaks of binding it is describing the act of tying, locking or bringing something under obligation to authority. Typically, when the sanctioned believer moves in the power of binding, they make declarations against entities in the kingdom of Satan, demanding them to be "bound" from being effective in the lives of men and situations. Loosing in the Greek is the word *lyo* which means to *release, untie, unbind, dismiss, dissolve, break up, or destroy.* When we loose something, what we are doing is making declarations that demand the release of Kingdom principles and virtues of God.

Another important fact is that binding, loosing and rebuking must always be done in the name of Jesus and can only be done by two agents in the earth realm; believers and Kingdom Authorities. Binding, loosing and rebuking can be effectively done "in the name of Jesus" or by His authority. The believer does not have the power to bind, loose, or rebuke spiritual wickedness by their own name. The authority given to the believer is directly connected to our Lord and Savior Jesus Christ and therefore must be done in His Name. The believer can make a declaration to evil spirits such as, "**In the name of Jesus**, I bind you spirit of sickness!" Thus, the believer must call on the name of Jesus in order for spiritual wickedness to adhere to their words. When this declaration is made in faith, the enemy will be bound. The believer can also loose or release something that has been bound such as healing, strength, anointing, or joy. When the enemy binds these virtues, the believer has the power to release them by making a declaration, **"In the name of Jesus**, I command the spirit of healing, strength, anointing, or joy to be loosed in my life!" This declaration will release these virtues into the area designated by the believer.

The believer becomes an agent of God when they are connected with God through a relationship. A believer can also access power with God through a repented heart. When a person has a repented heart, although they are not currently in good standing with God, their repentance becomes the doorway to power with God. Thus, when that person calls on the name of Jesus, He will hear them. **Romans 10:13** says *"For whosoever shall call upon the name of the Lord shall be saved."* When we use the name of Jesus, we are not declaring anything by our own authority, but by the authority of the supreme God of the universe.

The other agent that has the power to bind, loose or rebuke is a person given authority by Jesus Himself to execute judgment in the earth realm. Thus, a Kingdom Authority is someone holding a sanctioned ordination or position such as a bishop, pastor, apostle, evangelist, teacher, prophet or other authority within the Kingdom. Please note that I am not validating the use of any of these titles, but giving an example of the types of titles that some ordained authorities might possess depending on their denomination or Christian sect. These authorities can make a declaration of binding, loosing or rebuking because they are operating in apostolic authority as the direct agent and voice of God in the earth. These people have been sent and therefore bare the same authority as the sender, Jesus Christ. These authorities are similar to governors, mayors, and ambassadors of God. They can make statements such as, "Spirit of sickness, **I BIND** you!" When an authority doesn't specifically say in the name of Jesus, it doesn't mean that they are not operating under His authority. It simply means that as an authority, their words have been sanctioned as an expression directly from God. The title is not as important as the direct authority given them to make executive declarations on behalf of the Kingdom of God. Normally, this declaration of binding is followed by the statement "in the name of Jesus." In the like manner, these authorities have the power to loose someone or something. A declaration can be made, "**I loose** the spirit of authority, prosperity, and strength!" This declaration would release an individual to be able to receive authority, prosperity and strength. The second types of agents are basically God's principalities in the earth realm. Only principalities can bind principalities. Thus, layman believers must always realize that they can only bind, loose and rebuke under the covering of our Lord and Savior Jesus Christ. Kingdom Authorities must make sure that they have been sanctioned to speak on behalf of the Kingdom or serious consequence will happen.

Once again, binding and loosing, is an act done by those whom God has given authority to by the power of the Holy Ghost. All believers have the power to enter into the strength of binding and loosing, but they must be under the authority of God. There are many in the Body of Christ, conducting ministry without being under a spiritual covering. These people are in rebellion and are operating under the power of Satan, because as discussed earlier, rebellion is as the sin of witchcraft and detestable to God. Without being connected to a sanctioned covering, these people are operating in witchcraft which is made to look like the power of God. Satan's kingdom will only recognize the authority sanctioned by God. There is power in the name of Jesus by itself. Someone theoretically could see some powerful results just by using the name. But there are some demons that will only recognize someone using the name in connection to sanctioned authority. One could use a fake I.D. to get access into a lot of places. But when that person goes into an official building or is subjected to further investigation, the fake I.D. will be exposed and that person will be under heavy penalty. The same is true of binding and loosing. This is why Jesus told the disciples in **Matthew 7:21-23**, *"Not everyone that saith unto me, Lord, Lord, shall enter into the kingdom of heaven; but he that doeth the will of my Father which is in heaven. Many will say to me in that day, Lord, Lord, have we not prophesied in thy name? and in thy name have cast out devils? and in thy name done many wonderful works? And then will I profess unto them, I never knew you: depart from me, ye that work iniquity"*. The focus in this text is the *"will of the father"*. Trying to do a work for

God with a fake I.D. will never suffice and will ultimately lead to serious consequences. An example of this important concept is in the book of Acts.

In **Acts 19:13** states, *"Then certain of the vagabond Jews, exorcists, took upon them to call over them which had evil spirits the name of the Lord Jesus, saying, We adjure you by Jesus whom Paul preacheth"*. The key here is that the men who were going around casting out demons are called here, "vagabonds". That means that they were wanderers and not in connection with sanctioned authority. Once again reader, binding and loosing is not a weapon that should be used by those who are not sanctioned by God. The text continues in verse **14** and **15** to say, *"And there were seven sons of one Sceva, a Jew, and chief of the priests, which did so. And the evil spirit answered and said, Jesus I know, and Paul I know; but who are ye?"* This evil spirit recognized that these men were not sanctioned by Jesus to use His name. The response of this demon here is deceiving, because at first glance it would seem as though he was recognizing Jesus and Paul as co-equals as it pertains to authority. But what this demon was expressing was recognition of the power of the name of Jesus and the authority given to Paul to use the name. It is also significant that when these sons spoke to the demon, that the demon spoke back in defiance. Anytime a demon doesn't acknowledge or adhere to the one binding or loosing, it is a sign that God has not sanctioned the individual to operate under His authority in that instance or that the person in need of deliverance doesn't have the faith to receive from God. These men were deceived into thinking that using Paul's name in conjunction with Jesus' name would give them authority over demonic forces. There are many today that think that because they know a "big" preacher or attend a certain church, that they have power with God. But in order to move in the power of binding and loosing you must have a personal relationship with God for yourself. When we command a stronghold to be bound, it will be bound based on our connection to God. **Verse 16** shows us the ultimate result of the unsanctioned use of the weapon of binding and loosing. *"And the man in whom the evil spirit was leaped on them, and overcame them, and prevailed against them, so that they fled out of that house naked and wounded."* This demon possessed man was made supernaturally strong because of the evil spirit that was controlling him. He was able to overtake seven men and cause them to run out of the house. Yet, if these men would have had the power to bind the strong man, they would have been able to take over the house and set the man free.

REBUKING

Rebuking is in the same family as binding and loosing. Yet, the way some in Christendom propose to use rebuking is sometimes not in line with its designated purpose. Rebuking means to *indict, charge sharply, tax with a fault, or censor.* Thus, when we rebuke the devil we are openly declaring that we acknowledge his movements and that we declare his activity and presence censored from being effective. Mark gives us an interesting example of how the child of God can use rebuking to help deliver someone who is struggling with the forces of darkness. In **Mark 9:25**, the conclusion of a serious situation of a demon possessed boy is noted. It states, *"When Jesus saw that the people came running together,* **he rebuked the foul spirit,** *saying unto him, [Thou] dumb and deaf spirit,* **I charge thee,** *come out of him, and enter no more into him."* Note that Jesus rebuked the spirit first. When Jesus censored the spirit, it blocked that spirit's ability to speak or express itself through the outburst, foaming, and suicidal behaviors the boy was exhibiting. Next, Jesus charged the spirit to come out. Jesus executed temporary judgment against the demon; removing him from the vessel (the boy), doomed to wander until finding another vessel to possess. Jesus is very clear in commanding the spirit to leave and enter no more. When you rebuke a devil, it is important to give them a directive. They must be sent somewhere and be given a command. If they are not given a command they will hover and wait for another opportunity to express themselves.

This truth is seen in another example of scripture. Peter confronted Jesus, trying to block Him from going to the cross. Peter had just made an awesome declaration of who Jesus was (and is), but allowed Satan to speak through Him. Satan slipped into the mind of Peter, causing him to attempt to rebuke Jesus. **Matthew 16:22-23 states,** *"Then Peter took him, and began to rebuke him, saying, Be it far from thee, Lord: this shall not be unto thee. But he turned, and said unto Peter, Get thee behind me, Satan: thou art an offence unto me: for thou savourest not the things that be of*

God, but those that be of men." Satan, through the mouth of Peter tried to censor Jesus from speaking prophetically about His death, burial and resurrection, and from heading toward the cross that He would ultimately bear. Satan tried to use the relationship between Peter and Jesus to cause Jesus to have second thoughts about going to the cross. Jesus recognizes immediately that Peter was not speaking, but Satan was. Peter gave a frivolous rebuke, but Jesus showed His power over the enemy by speaking directly to him. Note that He gave Satan a directive, "get thee behind me". That means, get out of my future. Satan was still present, but he was not in front of Jesus to block Him. Believer, when we rebuke a spirit, we are censoring their words, thoughts and effectiveness. They must get behind a believer walking in authority.

Note another example in scripture concerning the power to rebuke. **Luke 4:41** states, *"And devils also came out of many, crying out, and saying, Thou art Christ the Son of God. And he rebuking [them] suffered them not to speak: for they knew that he was Christ."* Demons recognize and acknowledge the presence and power of Jesus. Demons must come to attention in God's presence. This should be noted and taken very seriously by the believer. If the believer wants to have power to cast out demons, they must walk in the presence of God. These demons were coming out without being cast out. The presence was enough to cause them to come out of people. The passage doesn't specify the demons by their distinction or identity, but it doesn't matter when Jesus is present. Whatever the demon or evil spirit is, it will submit to the power of God. Jesus rebuked the demons, which means He censored them. He didn't permit those demons to speak, because they would have started controversy among Jesus' enemies, causing them to attempt to kill Him before His time. Therefore, when we bind, loose or rebuke demons, we do it all under the authority of God, in the name of Jesus.

Discussions, Reflections and Activities

1. Give three scriptures that support the power of Jesus' name.

2. Why does Satan hate Jesus and His name?

3. Give two examples of a misuse of the name of Jesus in scripture.

4. What does it mean to rebuke?

5. Discuss some demon spirits that need to be bound and discuss personal examples of the effectiveness of using the name of Jesus. What was the situation that required the use of the name of Jesus? What was the outcome? How do you plan to use the name of Jesus in the future?

Notes:

"Let God Arise, let His enemies be scattered: Let them also that hate him flee before Him"

Psalms 68:1

Chapter 12

PRAISE, WORSHIP & TESTIMONIES

Praise and Worship is a weapon that is extremely important in spiritual warfare and has gained much popularity within the Body of Christ in recent years. There was a time in which Pentecostals were one of very few denominations that understood the significance of praise and worship as a weapon and act of public worship. But now, this revelation has spread throughout the whole Body of Christ which makes it a viable force against the kingdom of Satan. While praise and worship has gained much attention in recent years, it is still often misused and misunderstood. Praising essentially is to make statements that are positive about our God based on all that He has done. Worship is generally accepted as the act of acknowledging the essence of God, which is expressed by adoring His distinct characteristics. Praise in Hebrew carries different meanings for the actions done to exhibit praise. Pastor Steve Pruit is a world renowned song writer and specialist on the topic of praise and worship. He lists eight prominent words used for praise and their definitions on his exciting website *justworship.com:*

Barak-To kneel or bow, to give reverence to God as an act of adoration, implies a continual conscious giving place to God, to be a tuned to him and his presence.

Psalm 34:1 *"I will **bless** the Lord at all times; His praise shall continually be in my mouth."*

Psalm 100:4 *"Enter into his gates with thanksgiving, and into his courts with praise. Be thankful to him, and **bless** his name."*

Guwl-To spin around, under the influence of any violent emotion.

Psalm 118:24 *"This is the day the Lord has made; We will **rejoice** and be glad in it."*

Hallal-To praise, to make a show or rave about, to glory in or boast upon, to be clamorously foolish about your adoration of God.

[260]

Psalm 22:23 *"You who fear the Lord, **praise** him! All you descendants of Jacob, glorify him, and fear him, all you offspring of Israel!"*

Shachah-To depress or prostrate in homage or loyalty to God, bow down, fall down flat.

Psalm 29:2 *"Give unto the Lord the glory due to his name; **Worship** the Lord in the beauty of holiness."*

Psalm 95:6 *"Oh come, let us **worship** and bow down; Let us kneel before the Lord our maker."*

Tehillah-to sing hallal, a new song, a hymn of spontaneous praise glorifying God in song.

Psalm 34:1 *"I will bless the Lord at all times; His **praise** shall continually be in my mouth."*

Psalm 40:3 *"He has put a new song in my mouth -- **praise** to our God; Many will see it and fear, and will trust in the Lord."*

Psalm 149:1 *"Praise the Lord! Sing to the Lord a new song, and his **praise** in the assembly of saints."*

Todah-An extension of the hand, avowal, adoration, a choir of worshipers, confession, sacrifice of praise, thanksgiving.

Psalm 69:30 *"I will praise the name of God with a song, and will magnify him with **thanksgiving**."*

[261]

Psalms 100:4 *"Enter into his gates with **thanksgiving**, and into his courts with praise. Be thankful to him, and bless his name."*

Yadah-To use, hold out the hand, to throw (a stone or arrow) at or away, to revere or worship (with extended hands, praise thankful, thanksgiving).

Psalm 61:8 *"So I will sing **praise** to your name forever, that I may daily perform my vows."*

Zamar-To touch the strings or parts of a musical instrument i.e. play upon it, to make music accompanied by the voice, to celebrate in song and music, give praise, sing forth praises, psalms.

Psalm 66:2 *"**Sing** out the honor of his name; Make his praise glorious."*[17]

These words exemplify the acts of praise and worship, and give us an understanding of the type of expressions God loves. Praise and worship should be done together. There is no need to further explore all the logistics and semantics that come along with trying to define what praise and worship is. To do this, is to miss the spirit in which praise and worship must be done. Praise and worship should be expressed and conducted because God is worthy of it all.

---

[17] www.justworship.com/hebrewpraisewords

One of the most popular stories in scripture is found in John 4:1-30. It is the story of Jesus meeting the Samaritan woman at the well. This was a divine meeting orchestrated to illustrate the meeting of the Lord and His body (The Church), being symbolized by this adulterous woman who goes to a well and meets her Savior, the husband of the Church. In scripture, it was common for men to meet their wives around wells and water, thus this story gives us a picture of a divine meeting which changes the life of this woman. After a short discourse, the woman seemed to be offended at the Lord's interaction with her, seeing that He was a Jew and she was but a Samaritan. When Jesus exposed her adultery, she immediately knew that He was at least a prophet and changed the conversation from her inadequacies to an ongoing controversy between Jews and Samaritans. The issue was essentially this, "Where does worship take place?" If the question of where is asked, then we must also ask "what is worship?" and "with what do we worship?" Jesus addresses this issue in **John 4:22-24** *"Ye worship ye know not what: we know what we worship: for salvation is of the Jews. But the hour cometh, and now is, when the true worshippers shall worship the Father in spirit and in truth: for the Father seeketh such to worship him. God is a Spirit: and they that worship him must worship him in spirit and in truth. "*

Reader, this text finds the central idea behind worshipping as a tool for worship and warfare. First, worship must be done within the confines of a true relationship with the Eternal God. It cannot be faked, conjured up, imitated or fabricated. Jesus tells her, *"Ye worship ye know not what"*. What He was saying was, "You cannot worship what you do not know". Thus, the quantity of your worship is in direct correlation with the relationship you have with God and what you know Him to be. This does not discount anyone's worship. God desires worship from those who know a lot about Him and those who know very little about Him. It only signifies that a person with limited knowledge can only give God worship in proportion to the depth of their relationship with Him. There are many gifted people in the Church, singing and playing instruments better than some of the world's greatest, but if they do not have a relationship with God, the notes they sing, or chords they play are useless sounds released into the atmosphere like a vapor, beginning heavy but eventually evaporating.

Secondly, Jesus points out to the woman that there is a distinction between worshippers and true worshippers. Worship in most churches has become bodily exercise; going through physical motions in an attempt to elicit some power from God. I noticed on one major Christian network that people were hired to stand in the back of a singer and dance around and make lots of noise in order to give the perception that God was moving in the building. Yet, the Father is not just looking for worshippers who come together and express actions that are not connected to a relationship with Him. He is looking for worship from people who have a true relationship with Him. It is this type of worship that is dangerous to the kingdom of Satan. The glorification of God will always elicit a response from heaven.

Lastly, Jesus makes it very clear that cognitive ascensions and declaration of intellect of who God is will not suffice in creating true worship. Jesus states, *"God is a Spirit: and they that worship him must worship him in spirit and in truth"*. Truth must be connected to spirit in order for the formula of worship to be complete. Satan is not scared of large gatherings that profess glossy words for God's power and identity. Satan understands more than most of us that our war is not natural, for we wrestle not against flesh and blood. In order for a shift to take place in the spirit, the children of God must engage in that which is spiritual. A spiritual people can engage in spiritual worship. This type of worship is not predicated upon volume, activity or ritual. The power of worship that Jesus is speaking of is predicated upon the sincerity of a people who are in relationship with their God through His spirit. All fabrications and expressions of the flesh are null and void in spiritual warfare. No wonder our churches are full of people and not power. No wonder people are not being saved through the praise and worship experience at many of our churches. No wonder people in the Body of Christ require so must external stimuli in order to feel connected with God in worship. No wonder the "worship experience" of our churches has become the focus of comedy relief programs where jokes are made about people shouting around, yet not living sincere before God. A carnal people can only imitate worship, but cannot truly offer God worship. Worship is our duty to God, and is the catalyst for great warfare. When God is exalted, He will rise to fight on behalf of His children.

Psalms 138:1-3 states, *"I will praise thee with my whole heart: before the gods will I sing praise unto thee. I will worship toward thy holy temple, and praise thy name for thy lovingkindness and for thy truth: for thou hast magnified thy word above all thy name. In the day when I cried thou answeredst me, and strengthenedst me with strength in my soul."* Please note that David praises from his heart which is the only way praise should be given to our God. It is also done in unison with the heavenly hosts (gods). His praise is expressed with worship toward the temple. Thus, praise and worship is not only a private action, but should also be done in the congregation of believers. David's praise and worship is expressed in this passage because of God's love and His truth, but also because of the immutable nature of God's word and nature.

For the purposes of our discussion, praise and worship must be understood as a weapon. God has sanctioned that praise and worship would be the catalyst to cause the Kingdom to move on behalf of His children. Praise and worship stands against the wiles of the enemy and testifies of our faith in God and the belief that whatever He does is righteous and glorious. David says, *"I will bless the Lord at all times: His praise shall continually be in my mouth"* **(Psalms 34:1).** The declaration that God is sovereign and worthy of honor in all and any situation, is a direct attack against the false knowledge that the devil has blinded the eyes of this world with. The Bible says, *"Let God arise and His enemies be scattered: let them that hate him also flee from Him"* (Psalms 68:1).

Praise and worship is also a lifestyle. It is more than a 30 minute event that takes place on Sunday mornings. It is a position by which the believer governs their behaviors. Earlier in this book we discussed the power of prayer and fasting. Praise and worship falls within the same vein as these two in that it is a position that one lives in, not goes in and out of. Paul says in **1 Peter 2:9** *"But ye are a chosen generation, a royal priesthood, an holy nation, a peculiar people; that ye should shew forth the praises of him who hath called you out of darkness into his marvellous light."* God has called us to be a chosen generation. That means separated and unique from the world. He calls us a royal priesthood, meaning that our duties of offering up sacrifices, prayers, praise and worship is considered in high regard in God's eyes. He sees us as royalty. Finally, we are a holy and peculiar people. We exist and live in the holiness of God, which gives us the right and authority to call upon His name. But note that all of our qualities and characteristics are for the Glory of God. He says, *"that ye should shew forth the praises of Him."* Therefore, praise and worship is a lifestyle. When people come in contact with the children of God, they should immediately sense that there is a unique difference about them which is seen in both word and deed.

EXAMPLES

There are some examples in scripture that show how powerful praise and worship can be. In the book of Exodus Israel's first major battle against Amalek is documented. The significance here is the connection between the actions of Moses and the ability of Israel to prevail in battle. Moses as the leader had to take the lead in battle. But he isn't required to fight with the sword, but with acts of worship. The Bible says, *"So Joshua did as Moses had said to him, and fought with Amalek: and Moses, Aaron, and Hur went up to the top of the hill. And it came to pass, when Moses held up his hand, that Israel prevailed: and when he let down his hand, Amalek prevailed. But Moses hands were heavy; and they took a stone, and put it under him, and he sat thereon; and Aaron and Hur stayed up his hands, the one on the one side, and the other on the other side; and his hands were steady until the going down of the sun. And Joshua discomfited Amalek and his people with the edge of the sword"* Exodus 17:10-13.

The lifting of the hands is a form of worship and praise. One of the Hebrew words for praise is *yadah* which means *to worship with extended hands*. The fight in this text was against the nomadic terrorist-like people of Amalek. The Amalekites are a group in scripture that Israel had to fight over and over again because they would attack during times in which Israel was vulnerable. This is the way the enemy wants to terrorize the lives of humans and the Church. Satan wants to attack when people are vulnerable and pillage the

[268]

resources of the Kingdom. As long as Moses' hands were extended and raised, the children of Israel would win the battle. The key here is that the leader is in the position of worship. He is at the top of the mount. Leaders must be in a place of worship if the devil is to be defeated. Too often, leaders take an apathetic role in praise and worship. Leaders should lead the way for the people to enter into worship. When leaders don't worship, defeat is inevitable. The second key is that Aaron and Hur had the duty of making sure Moses' hands remained extended. That means children of God have to help others worship. The battle is "ours" and must therefore be fought together. We must fight in unison and in order. The third key is that Moses rested on the "rock", which is symbolic of Christ. Praise and Worship creates rest. Fear is removed, frustrations dissipate, and God is released to war on our behalf. When we are in a place of worship we are able to rest in faith and the knowledge of the power of our God.

Paul and Silas give us another example of the power of praise and worship. The Bible says in **Acts 16:24-26** *"Who, having received such a charge, thrust them into the inner prison, and made their feet fast in the stocks. And at midnight Paul and Silas prayed, and sang praises unto God: and the prisoners heard them. And suddenly there was a great earthquake, so that the foundations of the prison were shaken: and immediately all the doors were opened, and every one's bands were loosed."* This passage of scripture is one of the most powerful in the Bible. This passage shows us the result of engaging in praise and worship. Paul and Silas were thrown into prison. The Bible points out that these men of God were thrown into the inner prison and their feet were put in stocks. Satan will always try to lock the people of God in the prisons of this life. Yet, even though Paul and Silas were in a deep dark prison, Satan could not lock up their hearts and their mouths. When Paul and Silas prayed and sang praises an earthquake came. God will often send a natural expression to validate His approval of our spiritual expressions to Him. What Paul and Silas were fighting was spiritual wickedness who didn't want the gospel to go forth. These men fought against those spirits with the Holy Spirit through praise and worship. When they praised God, not only were they loosed, everyone else around them was freed. Our praise is so powerful through God that it will free people around us into liberty, freedom, healing, and the glorious power of the Kingdom.

In order to get natural results, we must war in the spirit. Our praise must be from our spirits. Our music must be from the spirit. Our songs must be in the spirit. And most certainly, our worship must be in the spirit because *"God is a Spirit: and they that worship him must worship him in spirit and in truth"* **(John 4:24)**. This earthquake was so powerful that it caused the foundation to shake. God will shake the foundations of Satan's kingdom through praise and worship. Not the walls and ceiling only; but the very foundation upon which Satan's kingdom is built upon. Therefore, praise and worship is essential to conducting spiritual warfare. All across the world, virtually every Christian denomination has caught the revelation power of praise and worship. Regardless of one's position in the Body of Christ, praise and worship is one area of warfare that is vital for all to participate and be effective in. **HALLELUIAH!**

THE POWER OF THE TESTIMONY

An area of warfare that is connected to praise and worship, and often goes unnoticed, is the power of our testimony. Remember reader, all of life as we know it is moving swiftly to the judgment. Think about that, judgment. Since there is going to be a judgment, there has to be a trial. When the Bible says Satan is the accuser of the children of God, it was not speaking figuratively. Satan is waging war against the children of God, putting together the defense of his rebellious position, and preparing his prosecution of the children of God all at the same time. That means that there is a trial in progress. What are the elements of a trial? There is a judge, plaintiff, defendant, prosecutor, and defense attorney. Believer, you are the witness. Your testimony is damaging to the kingdom of Satan and the case that he is trying to bring against God. He wants man to believe that there is no God. He wants man to believe that he is a god. He wants man to give credit to himself, rather than to God for all that is good. He wants man to blame God for the ills of this life and to see God as a restrictor of privilege and freedom instead of the giver of life more abundantly. *"Who hath believed our report? and to whom is the arm of the LORD revealed?"* **Isaiah 53:1.** When the hand of the Lord is revealed, a testimony is generated. Your testimony is proof that God is still on the thrown. Your testimony combats the false evidence that Satan is trying to mount against God. When people hear your testimony, it makes them move toward faith which is the key to accessing the power of God.

It is no wonder why the old testimony services that used to take place in churches have become "out of style". The enemy doesn't want children of God to be vocal about their experiences with God, which is seen in everything from the seemingly simple things in life, like waking up in the morning, to the great miracles or healings and protection from fatal accidents. Many church leaders have decided that a time set aside for testimonies is a waste of service time and should only be done in conjunction with a church leader's selfish motives of increased offerings or desire for fame. Yet, I submit to you that our testimonies are not only worship and praise to God, but are an indictment against the enemy and all of his works. My testimony expresses relationship, which has nothing to do with my goodness, but God's goodness. When I testify, I am a witness for the Lord and a witness against the enemy. I become the living proof of God's power and authority. My testimony worships God and also releases faith into the atmosphere which the devil cannot block.

The great theologian Johnathan Edwards in *Religious Affections* wrote, *"But the true martyrs of Jesus Christ are called his witnesses; and all the saints, who by their holy practice under great trials, declare that faith, which is the substance of things hoped for, and the evidence of things not seen, are called witnesses,*

Heb. 11:1, and 12:1, because by their profession and practice, they declare their assurance of the truth and divinity of the gospel, having had the eyes of their minds enlightened to see divinity in the gospel, or to behold that unparalleled, ineffably excellent, and truly divine glory shining in it, which is altogether distinguished, evidential, and convincing: so that they may truly be said to have seen God in it, and to have seen that it is indeed divine; and so can speaking the style of witnesses; and not only say that they think the gospel is divine, but say, that it is divine, giving it in as their testimony, because they have seen it to be so" [18]*pg. 141-142.* The power that comes to the believer from the progressive movement of seeing God, knowing God, and therefore speaking on behalf of God is what causes the enemy's kingdom to crumble. The testimony of the believer concerning the gospel is synthesized into a confession of faith that is not only based upon the truth of the death, burial, and resurrection of Christ alone, but also on the living experiences of the believer. The believer becomes living proof of the power of the gospel. God allows for situations to arise in our lives that require us to call upon Him. God doesn't leave any room for doubt concerning His delivering power. When you are delivered from horrible situations, great and small, it is a witness to the saving power of Christ. This practical life application cannot be disputed by the adversary. There is no room for guessing or soft statements that include the possibility of some other intervening force other than God. It is my experience with

---

[8] Edwards, Johnathan "Religious Affections". Diggory Press (2007) Goodyear, AZ

God that gives me the power to be a witness for Him, thereby becoming a weapon of warfare.

The Samaritan woman in John 4 shows how powerful a testimony is. She immediately went to testify of her experience with the Lord. **John 4:29-30** says, *"come, see a man, which told me all things that ever I did: is not this the Christ? Then they went out of the city, and came unto him."* This woman did more with her testimony than many do in their whole life time. After coming in contact with the Living Word, she began to spread the word. Her words were so powerful that all the people immediately left out of the city to come to Jesus. There was an immediate Kingdom exchange. A whole city was moved to faith. This is the result of true successful warfare; people will come to Christ. When people are not moved to faith and discipleship, true spiritual warfare has not taken place. Your testimony is deadly to the enemy's kingdom.

Another example of the power of a testimony is in the book of Revelation. John's revelation concerning the victory that God's people will ultimately win over the accuser is highlighted in the twelfth chapter. In **Revelation 12:11** he states, *"And they overcame him (Satan/Accuser) by the blood of the Lamb, and by the word of their testimony; and they loved not their lives unto the death."* The blood of the Lamb is the saving power of Christ and the testimony is the acceptance and acknowledgment of salvation as originating from the only true and living God. This is the connection that must be understood in order for your testimony to be used in spiritual warfare. It is the blood that has secured us the victory over the enemy. But the victory is realized when we testify about the power of God in our lives. Our testimonies stand in direct opposition to the lies of the enemy. The only thing that can shut down the lies of the accuser is the truth of our God. When you tell someone that you have been delivered, that Jesus has saved you, that in all you do God deserves the glory, and that there is only one true and living God, the enemy's kingdom is further destroyed.

Finally, the power of our testimony is expressed in the way we live. With all of the issues that face our world, people are looking to the children of God to see how they should respond. Contrary to popular belief, the Church of the living God is still a beacon of light to the world and must therefore live in the victory of our Savior, Jesus Christ. Economic, social, and health issues face our world as never before. There are new dangers around the world that are rushing us into the hour of our Lord's coming. Therefore, the way the children of God live is a powerful testimony to the power of God. Will we give into the pressures of the enemy, or stand strong against evil? Will we be a people of love and praise in the midst of trials, or be a negative entity, further exacerbating the situations that our world faces?

There are enemies of Christ who are working overtime in exposing the faults and short comings of people within the Church. News media loves stories about fallen preachers, indecent practices of peripheral organizations, and poor ethical and moral judgments of church leaders. All of the attacks, although some justified, are founded in Satan's desire to ruin the testimony of the Church, which diffuses it from being effective in leading men and women to God. Our lives should be a testimony that God is real, good, love, and pure. We should strive to live our lives so that when men and women see us, they will be moved by our perseverance, joy, patience and kindness. It is amazing how our lives can be a greater testimony than the pamphlets and tracks that we pass out to people. People don't want to hear about God as much as they want to see God in us. This type of testimony is devastating to the enemy's kingdom. *"Ye are our epistle written in our hearts, known and read of all men"* **(2 Corinthians 3:2).** When there are children of God walking in love and truth in the world, the world doesn't need a Bible; we are the Bible. This is very damaging to the kingdom of Satan, because he wants to keep men and women away from the gospel and the Church of the Living God. But when we allow our lives to be testimonies, people won't have to come to the church building, they will be exposed to the true Church, which is the believer.

Discussions, Reflections, and Activities

1. In what ways is Praise and Worship a powerful weapon against the enemy?

2. Think of three significant things God has done in your life. Write them down. What did you learn about

God through those blessings? How can you use your experiences to help other people?

3. Discuss three examples of how praise and worship was used in scripture to engage in warfare and defeat the enemy. How do these examples apply to your personal life?

Notes:

_____

_____

_____

_____

_____

_____

_____

_____

_____

_____

_____

_____

_____

_____

_____

_____

_____

SUMMARY

Now is the time for you to engage in the spiritual warfare that God has prepared you for. Throughout history, the acts of God have prepared the Church for the times in which we currently live. The enemy is raging and creating havoc in the land. Yet, in the midst of the confusion, derision, and anti-God stances Satan has intoxicated this world into taking, the Church has the power to rise up to a higher level of evangelism, warfare, and power. God is looking for believers just like you to take a stance of faith towards the word and gifting of God.

The first objective that needs to be taken by all leaders and believers in the Kingdom of God is to expose the devil wherever he resides. Everyone who holds a position of leadership in the Kingdom of God must take this objective very seriously. If the children of God are not aware of the vicious devices of the enemy, they will be absolutely defenseless against his tricks and kingdom. Every area in the Kingdom of God must be scrutinized and critiqued to ensure that none of the foundational characteristics of Satan's kingdom exist in the Church of the Living God.

There must be a unified effort taking place among Christians against the enemy. Whatever the doctrinal disputes are among organizations, there must be a common

[278]

ground found on issues that affect Christians as a whole. Divisiveness will never win the battle against the enemy. His kingdom is highly organized, and God's Kingdom has the power to become cohesive and effective in the spirit of unity. When there is a unified movement, the gates of hell will not prevail against the Church (Matthew 16: 18).

As we become unified in our engagement of spiritual warfare, the power of God's Kingdom will become evident in our communities, regions, countries and world. Unity is the key to make all strongholds and demonic forces loosen their hold on the lives of men and women. The Body of Christ will grow into an army that cannot be stopped or swayed when each of us takes a personal stance to do the will of God in warfare. It is my prayer that this book and others like it will help influence a spiritual change in the Body of Christ which will bring true revival and crusade back to all regions of the world.

Secondly, you must seek the character of God so that you can have the foundation to engage in spiritual warfare. Without the character of God, you will be entangled in issues of this world, which will keep you from ever taking up the fight against the wiles of the enemy. God wants you to be loosened from the bands of wickedness, and freed to move in the anointing that He has provided for all of us who believe.

Once the foundation of God's character is resonating in your life, you can begin to make decisions that are

consistent with the initiatives and goals of the Kingdom o
God. You will have a spirit like Uriah, who was a faithfu
and loyal soldier. You will begin to submit to delayec
gratification for the sake of the larger cause of Kingdon
building. Your connection with God allows you to make
warfare against the enemy, because whatever victory we
experience is not due to our own strength, but the strengtl
of our God.

Ultimately, you must use the weapons that God ha;
sanctioned consistently and fervently. The word of Goc
must be adamantly studied and mastered. This is the sworc
of the Spirit. All children of God must pray. A consisten
prayer life is of utmost importance for your spiritual life anc
power. Fasting is a weapon used to increase our spiritua
astuteness and clarity. As we mortify the flesh, God';
directions will become clear; giving us the victory over the
enemy. Meditation is a weapon seldom used, but is the over
by which God's power can marinate strength and powe
into your mind, body and soul. Praise and Worship must be
done in the Spirit. You must fight against the pressures o
Satan to become carnal. Carnality will cause you to operate
in the flesh as opposed to the pure heart of worship that onl;
a relationship with God can bring. My worship is not just ir
songs and music, but also in my confession of faith anc
testimony that I share to all those whom the Lord woulc
lead me to. Through the name of Jesus, we have all victory
Through His name demons will be cast out, rebuked anc
removed. Through His name, healing and deliverance wil
come to those who believe. We are armed and dangerous.

[280]

You are the tool God wants to use to make weapons of warfare. God will use you to fight the enemy and bring glory to the His name. You have to take spiritual warfare seriously. Spiritual warfare cannot be an option, but a priority. It is important that you don't get caught in the web of frivolous messages being promulgated in the trendy, self-driven church world. The Gospel message and priorities that God has set forth in His word must be your priority. Any preacher or supposed leader who would preach anything that would distract from the power of the Gospel is operating under a spirit other than the Spirit of the Living God. All weapons have been given to you for your defense, offense and edification of the Kingdom. You are the light of the world which cannot be hid. This is not the time to live a silent Christian life where Christianity is a fad. This is the time to start a movement in your life, your Church, your community, your nation and world that stands strong in the power of God, becoming tools that He would use to make warfare against the enemy. Let's engage in Our Warfare!

I will close with this declaration from **Psalms 68:1**:*"Let God arise, let his enemies be scattered: let them also that hate him flee before him"*.

Humble Servant,

Tobaise Brookins

References and Footnotes

All scripture quoted is from the King James Version of the Bible.

All Hebrew and Greek notations are from the Strong's Exhaustive Concordance.

The following references are cited according to footnote order and note standard APA format.

1. Encarta Dictionary: http://encarta.msn.com/dictionary/tool

2. Pressfield, Steven. "The War of Art". Warner Books (2002). New York, NY

3. Calvin, John. "Institutes of the Christian Religion"-Translated by Henry Beveridge. WM. B.Eerdmans Publishing Company (1989).Grand Rapids, MI

4. Bishop Henry L. Johnson. Bishop of the 16th Episcopal District-P.A.W. Inc. (2009). Fresno, CA

5. Tzu, Sun. (2006). "The Art of War". Filiquarian Publishing.(2006)

6. Owen, John."The Mortification of Sin". The Banner of Truth Trust. (2004) Edinburgh, UK

7. Lewis, C.S. "The Complete C.S. Lewis Signature Classics". HarperCollins Publishers (2002) New York, NY.

8. Nee, Watchman. "Authority and Submission. Living Stream Ministry (1988) Anaheim, CA

9. Douglas, J.D., Tenney, Merrill C., "The New International Dictionary of the Bible Pictorial Edition". The Zondervan Publishing House (1987) Grand Rapids, MI

[283]

10. Itiowe, Alfred. "Subduing Satanic Strongholds". Living Treasures Publications (2003). Enugu State, Nigeria

11. Mastrogiovanni, John L. "The Spirit of the Scorpion-Conquering the Powers of Insurrection. Morris Publishing (1992). Monrovia, CA

12. Luther, Martin. "The Bondage Of The Will"-Translated by Packer and Johnston. Revell (1957). Grand Rapids, MI

13. Warren, Rick. "The Purpose Driven Life". Zondervan (2002). Grand Rapids, Michigan

14. Stearne, Lottie. "Treasure in the Midst of Ruins-Birth our of Bondage". AuthorHouse (2009) Bloomington, IN

15. Stone, Nathan. "Names of God". The Moody Bible Institute (1944). Chicago, IL

16. www.jesuschristis.com (2009)

17. www.justworship.com/hebrewpraisewords

18. Edwards, Johnathan "Religious Affections". Diggory Press (2007) Goodyear, AZ

ACKNOWLEDGEMENTS

This book is inspired by God and is therefore a tribute to His power, not mine. He deserves all the credit and glory for this work. I magnify the God of eternity, who is the creator and source of all life. To the God that found a way to save all of humanity through His own plan and act in the person of Jesus Christ, be all Dominion, Honor, and Power both now and forever. I thank Him for the strength, mercy and grace to be able to move into this new dimension of ministry. For His goodness and hand of favor, I give all thanks to Him. May His blood prevail and His truth reign forever and ever.

To my Mother, Cinthia Brookins, Grandfather, Henry Brookins, and family members near and far, I say thank you for your continued support and belief in what God is doing in my life. May God bless you all. To Bishop Ernest Jackson and First Lady Doris Jackson, may God continue to bless you both richly for the sacrifices and kindness you have shown to me throughout the years. To my dearest Adrienne Jackson, thank you for all those things that go unspoken, but have been pivotal in my life. To Bishop Henry L. Johnson for your continued support, insight, and confidence, I say thank you. A special thanks to Angela Boyce and Boyce Enterprises for your undying effort and support of my ministry and this project, may you continue to prosper above measure. To Sharon Watts for so freely embracing this book and bringing it to a place of excellence, I say thank you. To every church, ministry, bishop, pastor and minister that have ever invested in, encouraged, or participated in my ministry, I say thank you. To all of those friends, associates, and children of God of whom I hold so dear to my heart, thank you. To those who gave me a hand. To those who extended their hand. To those who held my hand. To those who pulled me by my hand. To those who opened their hand. I say thank you. And to all I say,

"the Lord bless thee, and keep thee: The LORD make his face shine upon thee, and be gracious unto thee: The LORD lift up his countenance upon thee, and give thee peace" (**Numbers 6:24-26**).

[285]

ABOUT THE AUTHOR

Tobaise Brookins is an ordained Elder. He was ordained by Bishop Henry L. Johnson, diocesan of the 16th Episcopal District of the Pentecostal Assemblies of the World. He is a preacher, evangelist, teacher, coach, consultant, Christian education specialist and now, author. Tobaise Brookins was born in Los Angeles County. He began his ministry by founding a soul-saving campus organization called "Word of Truth Ministries" at the University of Washington in 1993.

Currently, he has a thriving and powerful evangelistic ministry. With years of evangelistic experience, he has become an authority on spiritual warfare. As an educator, he holds Master's degrees in Education and Special Education. He has taught special education students in the Los Angeles Unified School District for 12 years and has also taught in the New York Public School District. He has founded two Educational Programs; T.O.Y.S - Tapping Opportunities for Youth to Succeed (Northridge, CA) and B.E.S.T.-Bethesda Educational Services & Training program (Fresno, CA). He has recently founded The Gates Alliance which is a Christian programming, resources and consulting organization. These programs are only a continuation of his strong record of spearheading powerful church development programs, social programs and Kingdom connections.

"Our Warfare" is Tobaise Brookins' first major theological work. He has written four other Christian booklets: The Holy Spirit, Tools for Spiritual Warfare, The Garden Experience, and a prayer study guide called F.O.R.M. P.O.W.E.R. He plans to continue edifying the Body of Christ through Christian literature, programming, consulting and speaking. With a focus on Christian education and literature, evangelism, church growth consulting, social programs, and anointed teaching and preaching, Tobaise Brookins has an end time word for this generation. For more information, please contact:

Elder Tobaise Brookins

(818) 810-5777 or tobaisebrookinsministries.com

[287]

2012

W.O.E.

"WALKING WAR"

total submission to God
for victory in our
Homes, communities!
+ personal lives!

Lined up + ready for
to overtake our
enemy

Camoflouge —

LaVergne, TN USA
07 July 2010
188611LV00001B/17/P

9 780578 027029